Gendering Taboos

Gendering Taboos

10 Short Plays by African Women

Yanci

The Arrangement

A Woman Has Two Mouths

Who Is in My Garden?

The Taste of Justice

Desperanza

Oh!

In Her Silence

Horny & . . .

Gnash

Edited by

'TOSIN KOOSHIMA TUME, EKUA EKUMAH AND
YVETTE HUTCHISON

methuen | drama

LONDON • NEW YORK • OXFORD • NEW DELHI • SYDNEY

METHUEN DRAMA
Bloomsbury Publishing Plc
50 Bedford Square, London, WC1B 3DP, UK
1385 Broadway, New York, NY 10018, USA
29 Earlsfort Terrace, Dublin 2, Ireland

BLOOMSBURY, METHUEN DRAMA and the Methuen Drama logo are trademarks
of Bloomsbury Publishing Plc

First published in Great Britain 2024

A catalogue record for this book is available from the British Library.

A catalog record for this book is available from the Library of Congress.

ISBN: PB: 978-1-3504-0797-8
       ePDF: 978-1-3504-0799-2
       eBook: 978-1-3504-0798-5

Series: Methuen Drama Play Collections

Typeset by RefineCatch Limited, Bungay, Suffolk
Printed and bound in Great Britain

To find out more about our authors and books visit www.bloomsbury.com
and sign up for our newsletters.

Contents

Introduction

'Tosin Kooshima Tume, Ekua Ekumah and Yvette Hutchison

I have been vocal about the need for more opportunities and spaces that don't merely 'cater' for the black female voice/narrative/body in theatre, but ones that empower and back that narrative/voice in tangible ways, be it financially, or by providing resources, i.e. space, mentors, facilities etc.

(Koleka Putuma, South African playwright,
CASA reflection, June 2018)

The African Women's Playwright Network (AWPN) was established as a virtual network in 2015 to begin to address the issues raised by Koleka Putuma when academics Yvette Hutchison, Jane Plastow and Christine Matzke began researching *African Theatre: Contemporary Women* (2015), to analyse how African women practitioners, theatre makers, directors and actors were engaging with gender roles, inequalities, political and national issues in their artistic work. What became evident was that, while contemporary women in Africa are producing rich and vibrant work, it is hugely underrepresented in scholarship and curricula, largely owing to the difficulties involved in accessing the work and artists, as most go unpublished and are produced only locally. At that point, the only existing collections of plays by African women playwrights were *Black South African Women* (1998) and *African Women Playwrights* (2009), both edited by Kathy Perkins alongside a few individual plays in various single editions or anthologies, most from the 1970s and 1980s. This proportion is shocking given the size of the African continent and the prolific creative activity of the women on it.

These patterns of publishing and programming exemplify the ways in which colonialism continues to haunt the present and is being challenged by movements like South Africa's #Rhodesmustfall & #FeesMustfall campaigns from 2015, which criticized the systems that lock them into Western paradigms of knowledge practices and demanded complete shifts in paradigms, what Gayatri Spivak calls 'the task of epistemological engagement' (2012: 9) that involve new habits of thinking [. . .] and not just an addition of new things to think about' (Bala, 2017: 335). These epistemologies continue to be affected by how research is undertaken and disseminated and by whom, which artists' work is seen, published and taught. These decisions profoundly define what can or cannot be known, discussed, performed and practised now and in the future. At this point, Hutchison began to ask how to address these imbalances, access African women playwrights and engage their work more widely. Part of the answer was the creation of the AWPN, set up as a network to make space and create opportunities to actively empower the voices of African women within theatre, across Africa and internationally. One of its first projects was a call for new plays for publication, which resulted in *Contemporary Plays by African Women*, published by Bloomsbury in 2019.

Another legacy of colonialism is how people have been divided geographically and culturally in ways that have built ethnic mistrust, and resulted in ongoing barriers within Africa that limit pan-African collaboration, communication and access to resources. Prior to the AWPN, African women playwrights had no way to connect with each other across Africa or in diasporas, or access training outside of universities. Theatre programmers and educators also had very limited access to new unpublished work and female playwrights had limited opportunities to stage their work outside of their own regions or countries. As a result of the network facilitating community building, sharing work, masterclasses and mentoring online, including the invaluable collaboration of the Canadian Guild of Playwrights that funded CASA fellowships for women playwrights in Southern Africa for five years, and the staging of two in-person symposia in South Africa in 2017 and 2019, contemporary African women playwrights have become more visible to programmers and funders, and thus they have been able to access more resources, professional and personal support and career opportunities within Africa and around the world. And, most importantly, it has created a community for them to support one another; as Kenyan playwright J. C. Niala says, 'what this network is doing for us, in a way, is bringing down borders, recognising each other's work, meeting each other and supporting each other in ways that it's not possible to do otherwise' (2017).

However, in 2021 as Covid-19 eased, AWPN felt that it was time for its inaugural festival to both encourage and showcase new work. It thus ran a competition for new ten-minute plays (about ten pages each) with one to three characters that had never been previously performed, by women in Africa, themed around tackling taboo topics in African female writing. We felt that it was important to facilitate safe spaces to engage with important issues that impact on women, but that are taboo in many African societies. As a space of fiction marked as out of the everyday, theatre offers such a space.

We had seventy-five submissions from nine African countries which engaged a broad range of topics. The plays in this collection feature the top ten plays by African women from six African countries selected by three judges: 'Tosin Tume of Nigeria, Ekua Ekumah from Ghana and Katharine Farmer, a UK director and founder of the Theatre Laboratory. Of the ten plays, three come from Nigeria, three from South Africa, and one from Botswana, Ghana, Kenya and Zimbabwe respectively. It is worth noting that the other three countries from which we had submissions were individual playwrights from Cameroon, Ethiopia and Uganda. Given that, although there is no linguistic limit for the network, AWPN's participants have been predominantly Anglophone, of the twenty-five English-speaking countries, this is a small percentage of engagement and worth critical reflection. The list of African countries by GDP at purchasing power parity (PPP) according to the IMF stands as follows: Egypt, Nigeria, South Africa, Algeria, Morocco, Ethiopia, Kenya, Angola, Sudan, Ghana (World Economic Outlook database: April 2022); and by Trading Economics as being Nigeria, South Africa, Egypt, Algeria, Morocco, Ethiopia, Kenya, Ghana, Ivory Coast, Tanzania in the top ten, with Cameroon in fourteenth, Uganda in sixteenth and Zimbabwe in eighteenth place out of fifty-two countries (GDP/Africa). When excluding North African Arabic countries, the results of engagement for this competition map the economic power of countries almost exactly. This emphasizes the correlation between economic and cultural power and, if this is true for a nation, it is doubly true for women. According to the McKinsey Global Institute for business and economics research, 'Women account for more than 50 per cent of Africa's combined population, but in 2018 generated only 33 per cent of the continent's collective GDP' (Moodley et al., 2019). This suggests that African women are less able to access the means of production in all aspects of business, but especially so in the arts, which tend to be under-resourced world-wide. This both explains the skewed representation in the competition, festival and this collection, something we are both aware of and mindful in our work as we engage with the continent.

The plays have emerged as part of a very specific process whereby they were written and submitted for the competition. The top ten plays were then rehearsed and performed as staged readings by students in the School of Performing Arts, University of Ghana on 1–4 September 2022. The playwrights were invited to attend the festival and see their plays interpreted by Ghanaian directors and performers, hear the students' and audience responses, and attend workshops on aspects of writing and directing by international participants. They were then invited to revise their plays in the light of these interpretations and encounters. This collection reflects the result of this process.

'Tosin Tume, who curated the maiden edition of the AWPN Festival of Plays, was convinced that the idea of a festival where African female creatives could share their works and get feedback from a live audience would advance the mission of the network. Considering the fact that AWPN had held two gatherings in Southern Africa, the choice of Ghana for the festival was especially meaningful in our quest to spread our impact across the continent. Importantly, the theme of the festival, which focused on taboo topics concerning the lives of African women across the continent, was exciting. Tume, who chaired the adjudication panel, confessed that it was exhilarating to read the treatment of the theme, engaging with issues of identity, gender, sexualities, family relations and power from diverse but valid perspectives. Also seeing the actors breathe life into the words of the playwrights during the festival was priceless, as it made these women and their work more visible and enabled younger people to engage with them in supported and critical ways. The festival audience, which featured a mixture of genders, was forced to sit up and listen to African women sharing their authentic stories, and that was very fulfilling for the AWPN leadership.

The writers too have been significantly impacted. For example, Philisiwe Twijnstra, a South African writer, has said of her experience:

This experience had a critical effect on my writing process because the work was in its infancy. Being a writer amongst other writers who have gathered for a week, sharing work, watching, and commenting on one another's plays was a crucial networking event. Seeing my work staged by Ghanaians, two female directors and a cast from a different culture, as well as comments by women creatives from other African countries, affected my perception of my play. This influenced my process of questioning and rewriting it. A shift happened when themes such as social justice, political stance and gender issues redirected my writing goals. This was enforced by hearing how the other writer-participants spoke about their work and processes. Furthermore, this dialogue space has critically broadened my perspective on how to give and receive feedback.

(February 2023)

After the plays, we have an interview by Ekua Ekumah with Sarah Dorgbazi, who directed the ten plays in Ghana on this experience of cultural translation. We believe the voice of the director will be useful for other directors who may be interested in approaching the plays from different cultural frames.

We hope that this collection will provide an important resource for schools and universities looking to diversify and decolonize curricula and engage with short works for practical classes, performances and auditions from diverse cultures. It should be a useful resource for programmers looking for new work and scholars working specifically in areas of gender and dramatic criticism. We hope that it will widen the gate of what is staged, taught at schools and universities, offering greater perspectives on African women's experiences and views in a global context.

References

African Women's Playwright Network (AWPN), https://warwick.ac.uk/awpn, https://africanwomenplaywrightsnetwork.org/

AWPN-Ghana documentary film 2022, produced by the Theatre Laboratory, https://youtube/EJChgTmZads

Bala, Sruti. 2017. 'Decolonising Theatre and Performance Studies – Tales from the Classroom', *Tijdschrift voor Genderstudies (TVGN)*, 2:3, 333–45, DOI: 10.5117/TVGN2017.3.BALA

GDP | Africa, https://tradingeconomics.com/country-list/gdp?continent =africa, accessed 01/02/23.

Hutchison, Yvette and Amy Jephta. 2019. *Contemporary Plays by African Women*. London: Methuen/Bloomsbury.

Perkins, Kathy. 1998. *Black South African Women*. London: Routledge.

Perkins, Kathy. 2009. *African Women Playwrights*. Urbana, IL: University of Illinois Press.

Plastow, Jane, Yvette Hutchison and Christine Matzke. 2015. *African Theatre 14: Contemporary Women*. Woodbridge: James Currey/ Boydell & Brewer Inc.

Moodley, Lohini, Mayowa Kuyoro, Tania Holt, Acha Leke, Anu Madgavkar, Mekala Krishnan and Folakemi Akintayo. 2019. *The Power of Parity: Advancing Women's Equality in Africa*. McKinsey Global Institute, 24 November, Report. https://www.mckinsey.com/ featured-insights/gender-equality/the-power-of-parity-advancing-womens-equality-in-africa, accessed 01/02/23.

Spivak, G. C. 2012. *An Aesthetic Education in the Era of Globalization*. Cambridge, MA: Harvard University Press.

World Economic Outlook database: April 2022, https://www.imf.org/en/ Publications/WEO/weo-database/2022/April, accessed 01/02/23.

Yanci

Rukayat Nihinlola Banjo

Rukayat Nihinlola Banjo researches and teaches in the Department of Theatre and Performing Arts, Bayero University, Kano, Nigeria. She is a playwright, theatre director and actor. She holds a BA in Performing Arts from the University of Ilorin, MA and PhD in Film Studies from Obafemi Awolowo University, Nigeria. She has a bias towards gender studies as it intersects with film production and studies, cultural studies and the media. She has published works in the above-listed areas.

Synopsis

The play is set in a small rural community in Northern Nigeria. Hauwa, an ambitious teenager, is restricted by an age-long culture that prohibits women within the working-age population in a religious community from engaging in any kind of activity outside the home. Her disdain for the culture is revealed when she is pulled out of school and married off to Ibrahim, a university graduate and a teacher in the community school. In her revolt to change this regressive narrative, she resolves not only to get an education but to also liberate other girls in the community. With the support of Ibrahim, she tries to negotiate her existence. She continues her education at the community school by disguising herself as a boy, an act considered taboo in the community. She is labelled wayward and set to be publicly punished or risk being exiled from the community should she decline the punishment.

Characters

Hauwa, *a young Hausa girl, fifteen* (first played by Tracy Himmans)

Ibrahim, *Hauwa's husband, twenty-five-ish* (first played by Ernest Angmler)

Magariya, *Hauwa's mother, mid-menopausal age* (first played by Jemilatu Martequor Newman-Adjiri)

Setting

Living room

The sitting room of an old house in a rural community. It is scantily furnished with two old armchairs arranged in a slight arc. There is a door on one side of the room. It is sundown. Sounds of crickets chirping in different pitches symbolically tinge at a clash. The mood is tense. A young man in a caftan, **Ibrahim***, is seated in one armchair. A woman of mid-menopausal age,* **Magariya***, is seated on the edge of the other armchair, agitated.* **Hauwa** *kneels, holding* **Magariya***'s legs, weeping. Her head bowed in distress.*

Magariya (*casts a disdainful look at* **Hauwa**)   Well . . . your father has died from the shame of the taboo you committed.

Hauwa (*wailing*)   *Wayo* Allah! *Inna lillahi waina illaihi rajiun! Inna lilahi waina ilaihi rajiun!*

Magariya (*scoffs at her and shoves* **Hauwa** *with her leg*)   *Kin ga,* your tears are useless. You are a shame to the upbringing we gave you. To think that you are my daughter, (*beating her chest*) I, a member of the women's disciplinary committee in this community, is intolerable.

Hauwa   *Dan* Allah, Magariya, believe me.

Magariya   How can I believe you when you flout communal rules and committed taboos all because we gave you out in marriage to this weakling? Is he the one encouraging you to be recalcitrant? *Shegiya yar banza tsinaniya Kauai.*

Ibrahim   *Haba*, Magariya, she has only been attending lessons and nothing . . .

Magariya   *Yi shurun.* You should bury your face in the sand for calling yourself a man. (*Hisses and raises her voice to* **Hauwa**.) No woman in this community has ever been this irresponsible *ama ke kuma sai iskanci.* Are you not aware that a woman of childbearing age should be in seclusion?

Hauwa (*assertively*)   Why should I be in seclusion when I can be a teacher and train girls who will go on to impact the world, or a doctor and save women from the complications of childbirth, prevent and cure medical conditions of all sorts and severities that ravage our bodies.

Magariya   Every woman in this community has lived by these dictates. You alone have despised and spat on the respected tradition. Now, the word on every lip is that you are of easy virtue masquerading as a boy to attend the school, *yar daudu* . . . The height of taboo. What a shame. *Kunya*!

Ibrahim   There is no shame about a woman leaving the house, Magariya, times have changed. What is shameful is secluding women and preventing them from being seen and heard.

Magariya   *Auzubillahi*! Leaving the house and dressing like a boy attract grave consequences for a woman. Ibrahim, you think because you studied in the city you can feed her with all these visions of lofty dreams? You better wake up from your dream, two of you. The elders have given their verdict and it is binding on all of us.

Hauwa (*wilfully*)   Whatever the verdict is, it cannot be as torturous as this life I am subjected to.

Magariya   You will be publicly flogged as a deterrent to other future rascals. *Ku naji na*? Our tradition and religion do not leave room for waywardness.

Ibrahim (*angrily*)   Magariya, you mean you support this horrible action against your daughter? *Inna lillahi*. The community has decided to humiliate my wife . . . us? This will not humble us; it will only set us on the path to freedom.

Magariya   *Wayo* Allah! Is this a scheme to destroy the name we have worked to build and protect? Posterity will remember this act . . .

Hauwa (*protesting*)   For good, Kaka, for good. Oppression provokes rebellion. I want to create an identity different from Baba's. I will do this for myself and posterity.

Magariya (*hits* **Hauwa** *on the head*)   *Yi shurun*. Everyone is bound by culture and tradition.

Hauwa   You cannot shut me up this time. I am not everyone. I have read in Ibrahim's books that we all have the right to make choices. I assure you, Kaka, soon there will emerge a new culture for girls in this community and I am prepared to lead the revolution.

Magariya   La la la la! So, your mission is to mislead these virtuous girls. *Ba kid'ankali, walahi*! A bride should be busy taking care of her home and trying to bring forth children for her husband, not being unchaste. You were raised better than this.

Ibrahim (*calmingly*)   There is no cause for worry. *Karka damu.* We will bear children when and if Allah wills. Women have rights and dreams just like men, and they can be as successful as men if given the chance. Allow Hauwa to find her happiness.

Magariya   What dreams can a woman have other than ensuring that her family is well catered to? That should be the most important thing to her. *Ba haka bane*?

Hauwa (*kneels, pleading with* **Magariya**)   Homemaking is great but it should not stop a woman from being able to be whatever she wants to be. Please, Magariya, everyone has a dream in life, help me achieve mine.

Magariya (*irritably, she pushes* **Hauwa** *some distance away with her leg*)   Stop being stubborn. What does a woman need a dream for? After all, our husbands provide all that we need. It is tradition. Let them continue to dream for us.

Hauwa   What do our husbands provide, Magariya? The barely enough food or the nothingness with which they fill our lives? How many homes in this community can afford three meals daily? Some cannot even afford two. Yet, women are confined and not permitted to work or even go to school in the name of honouring some retrogressive tradition.

Magariya (*assertively*)   It has always been that way and it will not change now. You must learn to live with it. This tradition is for our good. We, women, are like flowers. We wither in no time. The most important thing is to be married and bear children for your husband. *Alhamdulillah*, you are married. All that is left is for you to bring forth children.

Hauwa (*sadly*)   Bring forth children, they say. They appropriate years of marriage to the number of children you ought to have had. How insensitive. No one cares if the body is ready, capable and willing to carry a child or how hard you try. Tradition is all that matters to them. Tradition my foot! (*Suddenly, she turns to* **Magariya**.) I refuse to sacrifice my life on the altar of your tradition. I have a goal, Magariya, and I will achieve it, with or without you.

Magariya   If you refuse the punishment and insist on doing your will, get ready to be banished from this community with nothing but the clothes on your back. I do not want this for you. (*Pleading with* **Hauwa**.) You have to let those dreams go, *dan* Allah.

Hauwa   I refuse to be complacent with this kind of life, Magariya. I refuse to be miserable. I was pulled out of school before I could complete my junior secondary because our fathers thought I was ripe enough to be married off and forced into seclusion. Where is fairness?

Ibrahim (*goes to* **Magariya**)   I am afraid this approach will further push Hausa to the outside world. Please, make a case for us with the elders.

Magariya (*ignores* **Ibrahim** *to address* **Hauwa**)   Listen and listen good. You will not be one of those city girls who abandon family in pursuit of their dreams. We value family here. It is the essence of our being.

Hauwa (*kneels before* **Magariya**)   Is that your fear? Is that why the community forbids women from even going to the market? *Kin ga*? Ibrahim has made a lot of impact at the community primary school where he has been teaching since his return from the University of Zaria four months ago. I want to be the hope and model for young girls, too.

Magariya *looks questioningly at her, shakes her head and starts to tap her right foot in quick succession.*

Hauwa (*looks up to affirm her stance.* **Magariya** *turns away from her*)   Yes, that is all I ask of you, of this community. So, forgive me if I want to pursue my dreams at the risk of being banished. It seems worth it to me.

Ibrahim   To live is to dream, Magariya. If dreaming here is taboo, then living here has also become taboo. (*Goes to kneel by* **Hauwa**.) I am with you on this, *Matata.* You have my support and blessings.

Hauwa (*stands*)   Allah *ya Isa*. He bears me witness that I have not indulged in any act of immorality as the elders and your tradition have claimed. All I do is obey the command of the Qur'an to seek useful knowledge even if it were to be at the end of the earth.

Magariya   How dare you speak of the elders in such a contemptuous manner? You were raised better than this. Does the Qur'an not also enjoin you to honour your elders? (*She makes to slap* **Hauwa** *but* **Ibrahim** *restrains her.*)

Hauwa   Do not push me to the wall, Magariya. I will no longer be a pushover. You, our mothers, are complicit in the atrocities against us. You have been silenced by insecurities and inadequacies shrouded in tradition. Don't they say all of us must change when our current selves no longer suit us? Now, go tell the elders that I, Hauwa, have made a decision and you need to come to terms with this reality. Enough of women being made invisible by this community. Enough is enough!

Magariya *stands in shock as* **Hauwa** *storms out on them.* **Ibrahim** *runs after her, calling.*

The End.

Glossary

Wayyo Allah! – Oh my God!
Inna lillahi wa inna ilaihi raji'un! – We belong to Allah and to Him we shall return
Kin ga – See
Don Allah – Please

Shegiya yar banza tsinaniya kawai! – You are only rascally
Yi shiru – Shut up
Amma ke kuma sai iskanci – But you are rascally
Yar daudu – Transvestite
Abin kunya! – What a shame!
A'uzubillahi – I seek refuge in Allah
Ku na ji na? – Do you understand?
La la la la! – What a surprise!
Ba ki da hankali, wallahi – You are senseless, I swear by Allah
Kar ka damu – Don't worry
Ba haka ba ne? – This is not true?
Alhamdulillah – Praise/thanks be to Allah
Matata – My wife

The Arrangement

Gisemba Ursula

Gisemba Ursula is an emerging interdisciplinary artist working in Nairobi, Kenya. Her work features live performance, cinema and writing. Her work focuses on the analysis, reflection and commentary on evolving African culture. She started her work on stage as the Assistant Creative Director in Spellcast Media producing cultural choral showcases and creating concepts with abstract chorus choreography. Soon after, she worked with Papillion Musa on his debut world music album, *Moyo*. With a focus on cinema to merge her different skills, she started as a writer-director for the short film *Stocoma* that went on to be nominated for the national Kalasha Awards and was also recognized amongst other local festivals. Her most recent project, *Beatriz, The Saint Prays*, was premiered in Kampala Biennale 2020 as a sound installation and later at Manyatta Screenings 2021, as the work evolved into experimental filmmaking. She carries on with her work moving through different forms and styles to test the boundaries of culture and tackle the different perspectives of representing African women.

Synopsis

A bride in her late twenties is set to be married. This calls for the respect of rituals and customs associated with the cultures of all relatives present. A dowry ceremony is held. However, every facet of her life is torn apart as the men led by an uncle scrutinize her lifestyle to determine what she is worth. Defeated after a brutal assessment, she goes on to be married. She stays hopeful that once the wedding is done, she can move on to construct a happily-ever-after which includes having children. Her body fails to comply. Each attempt at having a child ends in a miscarriage. Not only does this shatter her will to carry on, but it also strains the good will between the two families. The expectations set upon her as a wife start to take a toll on her as she suffers in silence. Meanwhile, the celebration of marriage through dowry seen before is slowly erased. She eventually leaves, frustrated at her loss, and childless.

Characters

Bride, *a woman in her late twenties on her journey from girlfriend to the stark reality of being a wife in a deeply patriarchal society* (first played by Ernestina Anokye Agyekum)

Auctioneer Uncle, *middle-aged man whose prime job is to convey the interests of the groom's side of the family* (first played by Adalba Agana-Nsiire)

Ensemble

(First played by Augustine Enninful, Ernest Angmler, Swanzy Menlah, Maxwell Esiful, Kobina Hagan, Jemilatu Martequor Newman-Adjiri)

Setting

A courtyard. The household of the Bride's family where dowry negotiations are held. Focus is on an auction block where the Auctioneer Uncle will be stationed. He will often break the fourth wall, pointing to his right to reference the Bride's side of the family and to his left when referring to the groom's side.

Time

The present.

Scene One

The **Auctioneer Uncle** *walks in from stage left. He walks up to the auction block at centre stage with an aura of self-importance. At hand, he has a gavel. He is adorned in a well-tailored ceremonial garment made of the African fabric 'ankara', which has become over the years the go-to wedding attire. He is sharp, filled with festive mood and anticipation as he prepares to deliver his big speech. He knocks his gavel three times.*

Auctioneer Uncle   A new daughter is a good thing. A new woman in the family is a valuable thing. Many times I wonder why Pharaoh killed all the first-born sons to destroy the lineage of the Israelites. The secret of continuity of life lies in the womb. There, generations are born and new blood-lines come to be. Kill a woman, and you erode the heart of a community. Kill a man . . . Well . . . We call the lion king of the jungle, but we all know the lioness is the hunter, the lion is the deep sleeper.

The **Bride**-*to-be walks in from the right side, stopping at downstage right. She stands at a distance, = from the* **Auctioneer Uncle***, a glowing spotlight on her and a moment of awe for her stunning attire and beauty.*

Auctioneer Uncle   Thank you for bringing your daughter into our home. This foreign home she will join, and two families shall become an extension of each other. We arrived as strangers, but we shall leave as brothers and sisters. From different lineages we came, but we will leave with each other's history and rituals cementing us as one. The rivers of love carried through the heart and soul of our son and daughter have finally merged, streamed downhill and settled in the lake of marriage. Our son has brought to us a coveted prize and, for that, let us begin a discussion amongst elders to settle the bride price.

Silence. The light dims on the **Bride** *but she remains visible.*

Auctioneer Uncle   Starting at ten cows each valued at ten thousand shillings. Do I hear eleven cows? Eleven cows?

Points to his right.

Yes, we raise it to eleven cows for her decent dressing, her admirable physique and for being silent. The mark of a good wife starts with how she expresses herself. We do not want our son stuck with a woman who is a local gossip, one who talks and talks yet does not listen. One who wakes with the birds of the morning not to sing angelically, but to cry and whine like a crow. (*Responds to an additional bid.*)

Twelve cows! Yes, she is well educated, a mark of respect for the women of today. Can she change a tyre?

Turns to the **Bride***; she nods enthusiastically.*

Auctioneer Uncle   Eh! I raise that to thirteen cows myself. She works well with her hands. Good hands that are not afraid of hard work make a successful household.

Another bid comes in.

Yes, my brother, fifteen cows you say. Oh, a Masters degree and PhD. Ah! So we have been in the presence of a doctor so far. Eh! Our son! We must empty our pockets at this rate. Sixteen cows for the PhD.

Another bid comes in.

Eighteen cows for being a working woman.

He seems slightly put off.

Twenty-two cows for giving us four children.

The **Bride** *suddenly interrupts.*

Bride   Uncle we agreed to have two.

Auctioneer Uncle (*appalled.*) She dares to speak? (*He knocks his gavel violently.*)

Auctioneer Uncle (*to the* **Bride***, stern*)   As we said, this is a discussion amongst elders. Twenty cows, that is where we are, my relatives. Our precious daughter shall give us two children within the first three years of our arrangement. We can only hope that she blesses us with a son first.

Auctioneer Uncle *starts to gesture to the left side. The tone shifts.*

Auctioneer Uncle   Yes, brother, a fine must be issued because the children have been living together before marriage. Our son was misguided by Western values and did not respect our customs. Your daughter was complacent and agreed to be part of this, nineteen cows. Because your daughter is spoilt, eighteen cows.

Another bid comes in.

I hear you, a woman who works shall never be fully attentive to her family and the household, sixteen cows.

*The **Bride** fidgets more intensely as the number starts going down. She raises her hand to protest. The **Auctioneer Uncle** ignores her; she withdraws.*

Auctioneer Uncle (*takes in a new bid*)   Fifteen cows you say, because she cannot cook. (*Addresses the **Bride**.*) How does a woman not know what the kitchen is for? Can you be trusted to feed a family? Are they supposed to go hungry or will you have children eating chips and nothing else. I am sure this one cannot even sustain a small garden with those talons on her fingers. Can you sew?

*The **Bride** is defeated.*

Auctioneer Uncle (*disgusted*)   Fourteen cows, if she cannot fix a button. What is the use of walking around educated and fixing tyres if your child walks around with a torn shirt?

A new bid comes in, even more devastating news than the last.

Twelve cows, we must strike it down for her lack of knowledge in tradition and failure to speak her mother tongue. Now, this is a matter we must clarify because the women of today are dancing to a different tune. Does she fully respect the woman's position as the neck? Is this one a feminist?

*He turns to the **Bride**. She nods a hesitant yes, but the message is clear.*

Auctioneer Uncle   Finished! Ten cows, final offer for your Miss Independent. Ten cows going once . . .

Pauses waiting for a rebuttal.

Ten cows going twice . . . (*Silence.*) sold for ten cows!

The **Bride** *looks distraught, but all has been decided. The* **Auctioneer Uncle** *knocks his gavel.*

Blackout.

Scene Two

The **Auctioneer Uncle** *will remain as a towering god-like voice-over throughout this scene. The auction block is still present but unoccupied. The* **Bride** *is still in her wedding attire.*

Bride   The laughter stopped, the dancers exited the podium, the moon went down and time for the party ran out. The sun came up and life quickly shifted to the mundane. We moved back to our . . . forbidden home and unpacked our matrimonial gifts.

She moves on to wipe off the lipstick, scrapes it off carelessly.

The grandiose rituals of wedding were finally done. We went back to settle into the monotony that is normal life, only now we were plastered with new labels. Recognized, respected labels – husband and wife. Titles that pervade the personal, transforming our identities – Mr and Mrs. Creating a new world of privilege designed to preserve wealth and hold the responsibility to create this nuclear family. Nuclear . . . Like an atomic explosion from false fission.

Auctioneer Uncle (*voice-over*)   Our precious daughter, you must work hard to ensure that our bloodline continues.

The **Bride** *proceeds to take off and kick to the side the bridal skirt. She is in trousers.*

Bride   Conception was an easy strike. They told us at the doctor's office that the first twelve weeks would be risky. It came as a subtle warning that meant nothing. Instead, we dwelt on the possibility of bearing a child. It called for celebration. Week in, week out, we walked around with tests called normal, stable, healthy. Glee was consistently plastered on the doctor's face. The nurse gave me general tidbits on nutrition for a new mother. My partner in crime held my hand and joked that the 'bean on the screen' would grow rapidly like Jack's beanstalk. It would be the first book we bought for bedtime stories.

Pause, shifts to address unborn child.

We read to you each page. We tried to teach you our language so that once you came into the world and opened your eyes, the puzzle of our foreign faces could be mediated with the sound of familiar voices. Reassuring you, welcoming you home.

She rubs off the lipstick on her cheeks with her fingers, but it only spreads around; her fingers are stained.

But I miscarry.

Pause.

What I carried I missed.

Pause.

The giggling in the doctor's room turned into a scolding silence. Five minutes, the doctor said, 'Something is wrong.' Ten minutes, he said, 'I'm sorry, I have to be sure.' Fifteen minutes, he could not find a heartbeat. Twenty minutes, the room dropped silent. He finally admitted it, 'I'm sorry – we have lost the baby.' A missed miscarriage? *A missed miscarriage*! Was the alliteration of the miss placed before me meant to reiterate and mock me of what I just missed? That the body could not sense its own self and created a missed opportunity?

But the world moves on promptly, I was sent back to the waiting room. Surrounded by ladies, all proud of their baby bumps. I had no new fun mummy stories to trade.

Making a mockery of the different characters who talk to her in the waiting room.

'Is this your first?' First, third or last, why does it matter.

'Have you been here before, this doctor is highly recommended.'
Recommended? For what?

'I can't believe I am one week due and I have labour pains
already.' Well, I can't believe I am having induced labour as a
'quick and painless option'.

We sat waiting, surrounded by beaming faces filled with great
expectations. We sat with a hospital bill driven up by all the wrong
reasons as everyone else sent quick texts of, 'It happens, don't
worry. You can try again.' My partner in crime stared at me. I could
only stare back because neither of us fully understood what
happened. We wanted silence but our phones rang and rang. The
family sought out answers we didn't have.

Auctioneer Uncle (*voice-over*)   A fine shall be passed to your
family. Five cows for a child has not been delivered within the
agreed time.

Bride   Like forget-me-nots, the memory of my bean dances and
floats in my mind. It fleets to the direction of nostalgia, lifted to a
heaven I will never know as I pick up the pieces from a new kind
of war.

Auctioneer Uncle (*voice-over*)   It is important that your daughter
understands that she must give us a son. Keep trying even when it
is hard – the ancestors surely will pour their blessings over a
resilient heart.

Bride   My resilient heart picked up the pieces from shattered
dreams. I got back into the schedule of feeling sexy, despite being
at war with my body, struggling to face the subtle betrayal of self
by self.

The **Bride** *slowly undoes the coat she has on top. Removes it,
underneath is a vest that hugs her curves.*

Bride   I stared into the ceiling as a loveless exchange ensued,
sinking into the heat of love turned disgust. I had never thought
moments of passion could easily slip into nothing but hollow
desires fuelled by checking boxes. With each thrust I pulled further
and further away longing to turn to the other side of the bed.

Is conception possible with such depravity? Well . . . Yes . . . The body knows not what emotions drive us to be, it's a functional entity, diligent to its tasks. Unless of course . . . When it's not.

Auctioneer Uncle (*voice-over*)   Daughter, the willing heart cannot fail.

Bride   What had been a distant dream turned nightmare the first time around, turned into bliss on second try as we passed the twelve-week mark. Weeks turning into months and we could proudly announce, 'We are having a baby boy!' We doubled down on caution and fear did turn into optimism. The phone rang incessantly as we passed the twenty-eight-week mark. Our life could only be described in that cliché wall hanging, 'Live, love, laugh'. All promises of marriage were almost fulfilled and relatives poured into our doors to shower the mother and baby with blessings for a first-born son.

But it would be six weeks when the bleeding would start and not stop.

Six weeks, at six o'clock when we would rush to the hospital.

Six weeks, at six o'clock, with six attendants grappling to save my failing body.

Six weeks, at six o'clock, with six attendants and within six minutes I would be unconscious and be put out of my misery.

Loud, insistent, disturbing ringing of a hospital ventilator beep persists.

Because I miscarry.

(*Pause.*) What I carried I missed.

(*Pause.*) I woke up to a small screen, dictating and spelling out a play on a future I had already seen.

The loud beep stops.

They said, I had to endure and dispel naturally because it is better physically. What is better physically at this point? I had to push. Push, I did. What came out wasn't the ironic new beginning symbolized by a burst of a child's cry as his lungs adjusted to the cold air of the earth. Instead, a resounding silence filled the room. A silence, so familiar, invaded every crevice of life once again. The self betrayed the self. My partner in crime, the hand that once held me, slipped into a world unknown. He disappeared into the silence for self-preservation. I disappeared into the silence to mourn. We roamed in the same home adjusting to the routine of living together but never existing as one.

Auctioneer Uncle (*voice-over*)   Pray to your God. Talk to your ancestors and appease them if they have been wronged. Ask for mercy because the good will of our families will surely run out.

Bride   Driving from doctor's office to doctor's office sounds like a hopeful escapade. But sometimes ambition wears out. I couldn't carry on. I simply could not . . . carry. The compassion in language slowly moved from 'Our precious daughter give us a child' to 'Your daughter is creating problems'. The hand that once held me, a partner meant for better or for worse, could not handle the worst. 'I'm sorry,' he said. I'm sorry is all he could say.

Auctioneer Uncle (*voice-over*)   Your daughter must report to see the elders within a week.

Bride   My time as a conduit to deliver the promise of a nuclear family ran out.

Pause.

Nuclear . . . Like an atomic explosion. Much like the cows exchanged for my womb, I was also driven back home.

Blackout.

Scene Three

We are back to where we started but in a less festive mood. Clearly seen by the change in the **Auctioneer Uncle***'s dress. A dull-coloured tan suit, and he seems less excited to address the matter at hand. The* **Bride***, dishevelled, stands broken.*

Auctioneer Uncle   Your daughter has left the family and we have taken the five cows left. She has chosen to desert the family and not honour our arrangement. Our son cannot continue to suffer if she cannot stay committed to the course. He must carry on in search of a new wife capable of giving him an heir. For this purpose, we shall retain all wealth and ensure he can find a new wife. There being no other stakes in this arrangement, the clan agrees to cancel this marriage.

He knocks the gavel three times.

Blackout.

The End.

Glossary

Ankara – African print fabric

A Woman Has Two Mouths

Chioniso Tsikisayi

Chioniso Tsikisayi is a versatile performance poet, speaker, writer and storyteller from Bulawayo, Zimbabwe. She was the first runner-up in the 65th Kenya Poetry Slam Africa Contest and was placed third in the Intwasa Short Story Competition 2021. Her work has been featured in numerous publications such as *Brittle Paper*, *Isele Magazine*, *The Kalahari Review* and *Agbowó*, with translations into Spanish and Italian by Vuela Palabra Magazine and Afrowomen Poetry respectively. This, her debut play, was selected for the African Women Playwrights Network's maiden Festival of Plays 2022.

Synopsis

After a woman's prenatal visit with her doctor, she discovers that she has suffered a miscarriage. Reeling from the loss of her pregnancy she finds herself in confrontation with her uterus about it and falls into an intense, in-depth conversation about fertility, sex, cultural practices and societal norms pertaining to the body, mind and soul of what makes or determines a woman's worth.

Characters

Woman, *nameless, representing the African women whose names we do not know beyond their roles as wife or mother* (first played by Araba Dansowaa Agyare)

Uterus, *calm, elegant, deeply philosophical and a little poetic with her gestures. She leads from a place of introspection and compassion* (first played by Bernice Nuna Quashie)

Vagina, *loud, expressive and very confident, provides most of the comic relief in the story* (first played by Maame Adwoa Amissah Quayson)

Original music for premiere composed by John Edmundson Sam.

Settings

A bathroom and a bedroom

The People Versus the Womb

Uterus (*to audience*)

I can hear it now.

Can you?

The sound of a distant drum beating in the void.

I am the void.

The drum beats inside of me.

Loud and luminous.

The rhythm and the blues.

A baby's heartbeat.

A life in bloom.

Beating

BEATING

and beating until . . . silence.

The heartbeat is gone and I know.

I know I have disappointed her again.

A distraught woman enters onstage.

Woman   I'm so sick of this. What is wrong with me?

Uterus   Nothing is wrong with you.

Woman   Who said that? Who's there?

Uterus *walks towards her*.

Uterus   It's me, your womb. Nothing is wrong with you

Woman   Oh fantastic, it's not enough that I've lost a child. I'm losing my mind now too.

Uterus   You're not losing your mind. A woman has two mouths you know.

Woman   Where's the second?

She gestures incredulously.

Uterus   Between her legs. The mouth that's kept hidden. The one that's not expected to have an opinion.

Woman   So, what? You're supposed to be a metaphor for the mind?

Uterus   Yeah, something like that.

Enter Vee the **Vagina***.*

Vagina   And I'm just the mouthpiece. Nice to meet you. Officially . . . Well, I'm your vagina but you can just call me Vee.

Woman   This is not real. This is not happening. I'm clearly just having some kind of meltdown. I had too much caffeine in the morning. I just need to lay down for a bit.

Uterus   Oh, honey, this is as real as it gets. We've been meaning to speak to you for months now. But you never give us the time of day.

Vagina   Exactly, it seems you're not all that fluent in body language. I have quite a few grievances to get off my chest as well. . . . Well, figuratively speaking of course because as you know I am a vagina and vaginas don't really have chests. But you get my point. I've always wanted to be a writer or like a public speaker or something. You know the ones that give like Ted Talks and stuff. I'm really very smart and super-sophisticated. I'm a clit with wit. See what I did there?

Uterus   Vee, would you stop rambling. You know in other parts of the continent they sew you shut.

Vagina   You're so hateful. That's cruel and you know it.

Woman   Okay, Okay. Stop bickering. MY OWN BODY IS TURNING AGAINST ME. This is absolute madness.

Uterus   No, honey. It's called democracy.

Vagina   I Just don't understand why you listen to those aunties of yours. Every single day you pinch my lips for no reason. If I had teeth, I'd have bitten those fingers off a long time ago.

Woman   Labia pulling? Is that what you mean? Listen, it's just something I have to do to please my – or should I say our – man and the aunties said I'd have a better grip in bed.

Vagina   Ha, look at the things I'm subjected to in the name of pleasing a man! If you stretch your mouth and pull your lips everyday, do you think that will make you a good kisser?

Woman   Oh, shut up. This is Africa. OKAY? Feminism looks good on paper. It's not practical for marriage. These people brought home cows. You hear me? Oh wait. You don't have ears either (*sarcastic tone*). So how could you possibly understand? The fact remains that *lobola* was paid in full. I was introduced to my husband's ancestors. Do you think ancestral spirits give a damn about some Chimamanda quote in a Beyoncé song? Do you think they're all sitting around drinking tea in the clouds discussing global warming and a woman's right to sexual pleasure? Get real. I still have to compromise even with my Harvard law degree so don't come here with your righteous vitriol.

Uterus   A woman is more than her reproductive organs. That's all we're saying. We're just parts of you. We aren't all of you and he promised in his vows to love all of you. Right?

I mean you're a whole human being. An educated, smart, dignified accomplished individual and even if you weren't all those things, you're a person with feelings who deserves to be cherished.

Woman   Please spare me the liberal nonsense. All a woman is is her body. Her ass. Her saggy breasts. She's a mannequin propped up in a glass window put on display for the world to pick apart before she expires.

Uterus   Well. It's sad that you feel that way but I'm not a ballot box for your in-laws, your pastors or your politicians. They can't debate over me like I'm a vending machine.

Woman   You're supposed to pop out babies. That's literally all you were created to do. That's the point of your existence otherwise you're useless to me.

Vagina   Well actually. I pop out the babies. She just incubates them.

Woman/Uterus (*simultaneously*)   Shut up, Vee.

Uterus   Listen. I get it. You're frustrated. You want to be a mum. You want to honour your father and mother's name and solidify your *muroora* status with the in-laws but, Sisi, *inini hangu*. I don't work well under pressure. I'm not a Chicken Inn Drive Thru. Okay? Since you have ears, listen to me very carefully. You're asking for a baby not a two-piece chicken and chips.

Woman   And what's your point with the fast-food analogies? Just cut to the chase.

Uterus   No, no, no. I've had enough. It's time I spoke up for myself. We just got off birth control. I'm trying to find my footing again and I'm asking you to be patient with me. Do you know what it takes to grow a human being? To form their little fingers and toes. To lay down that lining of blood and nourish their tiny bones, grow their fingernails and brain cells. And then strategically place your man's nose on that baby's face so he won't accuse you of having someone else's child. And I won't even begin with our egg supply. I'm working on a budget here.

Woman   If you don't give me a baby soon, they'll find another woman for him. If they haven't already. Someone much younger than me, more fertile. Someone who can give him five sons and a daughter. They're arranging a *Dare* with all the elders next week to discuss the idea of a second wife.

Uterus   Then he doesn't love you and I hate it when you talk about yourself like you're a piece of farm land. If he wants a son so badly, he should stop sending me X chromosomes.

Woman   Evidently. I'm a waste of space.

Uterus   I'm sorry that I can't turn pumpkins into baby carriages.
I'm not Mary's womb so I can't promise you Jesus. You heard
what the doctor said. (*In a remorseful tone.*) I'm not doing this on
purpose. Why would I kill your babies on purpose? I need help. It
hurts me just as much as it hurts you. I've made a mess of things I
know. I have to clean out all the blood and start again.

Vagina   Okay, ladies, let's not 'ovarryact'. GET IT? OVARY
ACT? HA! I'm hilarious. I'm a pussy with puns.

Uterus   Now's really not the time, Vee.

Vagina   But I think I have a real future in stand-up comedy.
Maybe after I've done a few Ted Talks I could write a memoir. I'd
probably call it 'Confessions of a Clitoris'. (*To be said with
dramatic flair.*) Then I'll speak about that time your English
boyfriend discovered me like David Livingstone thought he
discovered Victoria Falls. Ha, those were the days.

Woman   Ahhh, I was seventeen and I was stupid, okay? Why do
you have to bring that up now when I'm someone's wife.

Vagina   I'm just keeping it real, *sista*. Where's that excitement
you used to have? That zest for life? Where did it go? This
should be the most beautiful time of your life. The most
exhilarating.

Woman   Our honeymoon ended a long time ago.

Vagina   If he kissed me from time to time you wouldn't have to
pinch me. I just need a bit of romance. Some princess treatment
you know? I'm delicate. I'm soft. I'm a flower that needs to be
watered. You catch my drift? Have you tried kissing with dry,
chapped lips? It doesn't work, does it? My lips need to be
moisturized, sweetie, and seeing as I'm a very intelligent being, it
would be nice if he started with a little intellectual stimulation
before the deed. Penetrate the mind perhaps before penetrating me.
He should read Songs of Solomon for reference.

Woman   This is officially the weirdest night of my life.

Vagina   Oh, babe. The only thing that's left is to get my own TV show like Oprah and just yell out to the audience, you get an orgasm! You get an orgasm! Everybody gets an orgasm! How cool would that be? You'll have to excuse me, ladies, but we'll have to chit chat some other time. I've a business proposal to pitch and a whole lot of planning to do as a future Forbes list entrepreneur. You know what I always say, catch flights not STIs. Byyeeeee.

She exits the stage.

Woman   Is she high?

Uterus   Yeah, on estrogen. Lol.

Woman   I need to get some sleep.

Uterus   Yes, you do. I'm sorry once again.

Woman   I'm sorry too and I forgive you.

Uterus   This time when we try again, I'll try with everything that's in my power to hold on to that baby. I just need you to trust me and pray for me. Is that a deal?

Woman   Deal.

Uterus   Goodnight, love. Dream only of good things.

Poem to be read by **Uterus***:*

The Silence of Wombs

There is a bleeding in the silence of wombs,
A quiet stirring of the worlds between loss
And love.
The ebb and flow of bodies
From one generation to the other,
In orbit of each other's light.
And the lining in this space.

There is an awakening in the silence of wombs.
Fresh fertile wounds,
Freshly, cultivated tombs.

Pain becomes an inheritance
As does the joy.
As does the healing.
The widening of these hips
Like lips curve into a smile.
These genes do not lie,
They stretch wide across the waistband
Of this wasteland,

As
Barren hopes fill the empty barrels
Of dreams deferred.
We wait upon the Messiah to turn water into wine.

Poem to be read by **Woman***:*

Fermented Grapes and Fermented Ovaries

Fine like wine,
They say that's how we must age.
With no wrinkles in the forehead
Save for the few creases on your bum.
And a couple of lighting marks on
The thighs.

Fine like wine,
They say that's how we must speak
In sweet, agreeable tones.
Only indoor voices.
No shouting abeg,
A grown woman like you.
How will you find a husband
With your Malala wisdom?
Get a degree in the use
Of body language.
Let your hips speak for you.
But people are more forgiving to wine
Than to women.

They will not accuse wine of aging past its prime
But somehow when it comes to you
The giver of life
The carrier of seed.
Life is less kind.
Less forgiving.
Less accepting of fermented ovaries to fermented grapes.
Less loving of the fruit of the womb.
Children fall beneath vineyards.
The vines of truth entangle in the
Umbilicus of matrilineal heritage.
Fine like wine,
It's all a lie.
We are only as fine as the love given to us.
And better is the love we birth than the love we oath in the
    throes of passion.

The End.

Glossary

Lobola – Bride price
Muroora – Daughter-in-law
Inini Hangu – It's me

Who Is in My Garden?

Irene Isoken Agunloye

Irene Isoken Agunloye (formerly Salami) of Nigeria is a playwright, screenwriter and professor of African Drama, Women, Gender and Film Studies at the University of Jos. She has a BA in Film Studies from the Department of Theatre and Film Arts (1980), a Masters from the University of Ibadan (1983) and a PhD from Ahmadu Bello University (1991). She has a Masters in Gender, Women and Sexuality Studies from Georgia State University, Atlanta, USA (2019). She has received several international fellowships, grants and awards, including a Fulbright Senior Scholar Fellowship, Carnegie grants, a short course in creative writing in St Cere, France (2005) and a World Bank (Step-B) grant for Screenwriting at New York Film Academy (2012). Agunloye also won the IWF fellowship grant (2011–12) which enabled her to be trained at Harvard University Business School, USA, INSEAD Business School in Singapore and HERS Summer Academy at the University of Denver, USA. In 2019, she won a Rockefeller grant, for Women in Academy, in Bellagio, Italy. In 2002, her play *The Queen Sisters* received an honourable mention in the Association of Nigerian Authors' NNDC/J. P. Clark Prize. Agunloye's play *Idia* was shortlisted for the Nigeria Liquefied Natural Gas (NLNG) Literary Award (2010). Her plays include: *Plays for Junior* (1986), *Emotan: The Benin Heroine* (2001), *The Queen Sisters: Ubi and Ewere* (2002), *Sweet Revenge* (2004), *More than Dancing* (2003), *Idia the Warrior Queen* (2008), *The Naked Masquerade* (2013) and *Disposable Womb* (2019).

Synopsis

This play takes the audience through a journey that unlocks the secrets of a father, Maro, who encourages his wife to go in search of greener pasture in the UK while he remains behind in Nigeria to 'take care' of their adult children. Maro abuses his daughters and ends up in jail. His wife's very thought-provoking message, at the end, sends him to emotional damnation.

Characters

Simi, *a twenty-year-old girl, pretty, dark skin and agile* (first played by Bernice Nuna Quashie)

Maro, *Simi's father, a forty-five-year-old man, dark skin, tall and cheerful* (first played by Kelvin Andre Swanzy Menlah)

Noron, *Simi's elder sister, a twenty-two-year-old girl, pretty, light skin with a melancholic look* (first played by Elsie Catherine Amoah)

Settings

Living room, Kitchen, Prison

Scene One

Knock on the door, **Maro** *opens the door and* **Simi** *genuflects, greeting her dad. She rushes into the living room shouting.*

Simi   Mum, mum, mummyyyy . . .

Maro (*coming right behind her*)   Your mum has left.

Simi   Left, left for where? Just like that? I thought her flight is tonight.

Noron *enters the living room and holds her younger sister* **Simi**, *trying to comfort her, making signs with her hand. It is obvious that she is suffering from a post-traumatic numbness.*

Maro   The travel agent changed her flight last minute. They explained that if she didn't travel this morning her Covid test will expire, considering her transfer time in Paris.

Simi   Paris? (*Surprised.*) But her destination is London.

Maro   You are correct, but she travelled with Air France, so she has to transfer in Paris before catching another flight to London. Covid test regulations differ from country to country.

Simi (*stamping her feet on the ground and holding her head*)   Oh my God, this is so unfair. Why didn't you call me? My mum is leaving for London permanently to work as a nurse and I am not around to say goodbye. (*Shakes her head and tears run down her cheeks.*) Dad, (*with a feisty glare at her father*) this is not fair. (*She gives a bored sigh and folds her hands across her chest.*)

Maro *pulls her close and she rests her head on his shoulder.*

Maro   We kept calling your number but your phone was switched off. Your mum felt very bad too. In fact, she cried all the way to the airport.

Simi   Poor Mum, (*as she shakes her head*) life in this house will never be the same again.

Maro (*cuddling her*)   Stop mourning, your mum is not dead. She just travelled. She will be back in a matter of years.

As she struggles out of his grip, she gives him a defiant glare.

Simi   A matter of years indeed. That is so easy to say. Yes, a matter of years, working with strangers, walking to the bus stops in the snow, hunnnnn? You say it as if it is only five days. A matter of years. (*Re-echoes it under her breath.*) Dad, did your mum ever leave to travel anywhere? No. She was always with you.

Maro *moves closer to her and passes his hand around her shoulders to comfort her.*

Maro   It is okay, my dear, Dad will take care of you very well.

Simi (*arches her brows at her dad*)   Why is Mummy the one who had to travel in search of greener pastures? Are you not the man of the house? You never stop reminding us of that fact. It is your responsibility to cater to your family. Why did you allow her to go instead of you?

Maro (*rearranges his features and forces his tensed shoulders to relax*)   Enough of that. Go to the kitchen and fix something for our dinner. Noron has been busy all day cooking and helping your mum pack.

Grumbling, she leaves reluctantly, followed by **Noron**. *Light fades out.*

Scene Two

Night. **Noron** *tiptoes around. She is seen opening a door carefully, then she pulls out her phone from her back pocket and starts filming. Occasionally, she puts her hand to cover her mouth, in shock and surprise. Light out.*

Scene Three

Three months later. **Maro** *and* **Noron** *are seated at the table while* **Simi** *is serving them food. After serving,* **Simi** *pulls her chair* *closer to the table, settles down and begins to pick her food absent-mindedly.* **Noron** *keeps glancing at her. Suddenly* **Simi** *runs to the bathroom, and* **Maro** *follows her.* **Noron** *attempts to follow but her father pushes her back into her seat.*

Noron   Kpuhu, kpuhu (*coughing*).

Maro *and* **Simi** *reappear.* **Maro** *holds her hand and leads her to the living room.*

Maro   Simi, are you pregnant? Who is responsible?

Simi   Dad, I am not pregnant. I don't even have a boyfriend.

Maro   Really? A Virgin Mary has reincarnated (*claps his hands*). You are pregnant, my girl. You had better start talking.

Simi   Dad, how? Talk what? I repeat I am not pregnant. How can I be pregnant when I don't even have a man? I probably have malaria.

Maro   Okay then we must go for malaria and pregnancy test at the pharmacy down the road. (*Rises from his seat.*) Get ready and let us go.

Simi   Fine, (*shrugs her shoulders*) if that's the only way I can prove my innocence.

She enters her room and **Noron** *follows her. Shortly after, they both come out of the room.* **Maro** *is waiting impatiently. As they open the door to leave,* **Noron** *attempts to follow, but* **Maro** *refuses.*

Maro   Noron, you stay back at home. We will return shortly.

Noron *frowns and stamps her foot on the ground as* **Maro** *shuts the door.*
Lights out.

Scene Four

Simi *is lying on a sofa in the living room, crying and writhing in pain.* **Maro** *tries to pacify her, but* **Noron** *dashes out of her room* *and takes over, pushing her father out of the way. Using sign language, she orders him out of the scene.*

Maro   What is the matter? Oh my God! What is wrong with my daughter? What has happened? What did they do to you?

Noron *makes some sound; obviously angry, she gives her father an insolent look.*

Lights fade out.

Scene Five

Outside of the **Maro** *family home.* **Simi** *is sitting on a chair, looking very uncomfortable and in pain. The car is right in front of the house.* **Noron** *opens the back door and helps* **Simi** *into the car as much as she can. She shuts the car door and also locks the door to the house, putting the keys in her handbag.*

Simi (*raises her head and speaks with difficulty*)   What of Dad? Is he not coming with us? Are you going to lock him up in the house?

Noron, *with a wave of the hand, steps into the car, shutting* **Simi** *up as she starts the car engine. Lights out.*

Scene Six

Noron *opens the door to the house; she is devastated and falls onto one of the sofas wailing.*

Noron   She is gone ooo, my sister is gone ooo. (*She continues wailing and banging the sofa.* **Maro** *appears. He is shocked and confused to see* **Noron** *talking.*)

Maro   Who is dead? Where is my daughter? What? Noron talking? Oh my God, when did you start talking?

Noron   Your daughter indeed. Do you think I do not know what really happened? I saw everything. I filmed the whole incident. You killed her. The medication you gave killed her. The police officers are on their way. They are coming for you any moment now.

Maro   What? Killed my own daughter? What do you mean? (*His hands on his head.*) You mean Simi is dead?

Noro   You sprayed something on her that night that made her sleep and you raped her without her knowledge. What a taboo! Incest! Here is the video. (**Maro** *tries to seize the phone, resulting in a struggle between them.*) Don't try to destroy this. Even if you do, there are several other copies. The police department has copies already. The doctor said the medication you gave her to cause an abortion was poisonous.

Maro (*puts his hand on his head*)   I did not mean to kill her ooooo.

Noron   Tell that to the police. Dad, you did it to me years ago and I became dumb out of shock. I vowed never to let you destroy another person. I regained my speech the night you violated Simi, but I pretended to remain dumb so that I can see to the end of this. What will you tell your wife that you sent to labour for you? Your wife is labouring in a foreign land, working day and night to send you money, and here you are molesting her daughters that she entrusted in your care. You will rot in prison, Dad.

Maro   Noron, have mercy on me. I am still your father.

Noron   Your father, my foot. You deserve no mercy. (*Lifting up her right hand.*) Justice for Simi. You deserve to rot in the prison. Rest in pieces, Dad.

Maro (*tries to hold his daughter*)   Please, my dear, have mercy. Let us keep this as a family secret.

Noron   I have been silent for too long. I will be silent no more. You don't deserve mercy, Dad. Go to prison and ask God for mercy if He will answer you. (*There is a loud banging on the door from outside.*) There comes the police, please step out to meet them.

She holds the door open and **Maro** *steps out.*

Maro (*his voice is heard from outside, shouting*)   Take it easy with me. Don't push me. I am not a criminal.

Noron (*mockingly*)   Bye, Daddy.

Scene Seven

In the prison. **Maro** *is seated on the prison's visiting bench;* **Noron** *is seated opposite him with a narrow table in between them.*

Maro   Noron, I want to apologize again for all the atrocities I committed against your late sister Simi and you . . . (**Simi** *appears and walks straight towards him; he jumps and starts shouting for help.* **Noron** *jumps on top of the table shouting too.*) Warder, Warder, help, there is a ghost in the prison yard. (*Pointing at* **Simi**.) My daughter's ghost, help, help.

Simi (*tries to calm him*)   Daddy, I am not a ghost, I am not dead. I am alive. I wanted you punished for the crime you committed, so I planned with the doctor to tell Noron that I was dead. See, I am alive. (*She makes a 360-degree turn.*) Touch me, I am flesh and blood. (*Stretches out her hand.*)

Noron (*moves towards her, touches her and embraces her, shouting*)   This is a miracle! Unimaginable. Thanks to God.

Simi   Dad, this is your daughter Simi that you attempted to destroy. Here I am, not in the mortuary, but am alive, standing right in front of you. (*Searching her bag.*) Mum sent you a message through my phone.

Maro (*in a very sober and anxious voice*)   Please, what does the message say?

Simi   Okay here it is: 'Maro, I am shocked to hear of the crime you committed in my absence. I left you a beautiful garden, all you needed to do was to nurture it, by watering, and giving it the required passionate attention and special care so that it can bloom beautifully. Instead when you entered the garden, you destroyed it. I am here in a foreign land, labouring in the cold winter to build a good future for us, and there you are at home destroying that future like a bad hurricane. You are a disaster. Maro. Is this my reward for all my labour and years of sacrifice for the family?'

Lights out sharply.

The End.

The Taste of Justice

Martina Omorodion

Martina Omorodion is a theatre artist, creative writer and a researcher. She is a PhD candidate at the Department of Theatre and Media Arts, Federal University Oye Ekiti, Nigeria, where she is exploring the intersections of violent conflicts, womanhood and its depiction in contemporary Nigerian dramatic literature. Martina contributes scholarly articles to journals and writes short stories, children's stories and screenplays. She is a member of the International Association of Theatre Critics (IATC), the Lagos Studies Association and the International Federation for Theatre Research (IFTR). Her published stories include *A Mother's Cross* and *The Mask*.

Synopsis

The Taste of Justice explores the problems of child abuse, sexual abuse, gender-based violence and the complexities of the justice system. Miriam has been sentenced to death for the murder of her maternal uncle, the only surviving family she and her two younger siblings have left. Despite the hangman's noose dangling precariously over her head, Miriam has refused to speak or help her legal counsel put up a good defence in court in the baffling case of the murder of Chief Alasamaga. The play opens with yet another visit from the lawyer to Miriam's dark cell. Although, the lawyer has visited several times, Miriam would neither speak nor acknowledge her presence. This time however, the mention of her siblings Mercy and Moses being given out to foster care makes Miriam talk, and she reveals the trauma and abuse they suffered at the hands of their uncle. The lawyer represents societal perception of rape accusations against a powerful public figure. The lawyer is quick to cast doubt on Miriam's story, labelling it a desperate attempt to escape death and the ramblings of a lost mind. *The Taste of Justice* explores the normalization of abuse against orphans and other vulnerable members of the society. It depicts the denial and dismissals that often follow rape accusations in contemporary African society especially when it is against an influential member of the society.

Characters

Miriam, *an eighteen-year-old female, accused of murder and sentenced to death* (first played by Ruby Akuorkor Charway)

Lawyer, *a young male legal counsel* (first played by Maxwell Esiful)

Setting

Interrogation room

A dimly lit stage. The stage is built to look like an interrogation room. There is a single table in the room and a metal chair behind it, directly facing the auditorium. Another chair, this one a white plastic one, is placed opposite the table. It is the only thing of colour in the room and has been placed there for the visitor. The room is dark and the mood is dreary. A single naked yellow light bulb hangs over the table providing illumination into the room. The orchestra plays a sorrowful dirge to set the mood. Lights come on. A middle-aged man dressed in a smart suit and a lawyer's wig comes into the room. He has a black lawyer's gown over one arm and some files on the other arm. He drops the heavy files on the table and drapes the black gown over the white plastic chair. He looks around, turns and speaks into the dark room.

Lawyer Hello, miss. How are you today? I hope you feel better and able to talk.

Silence.

He sighs resignedly, and fidgets with the files on the table. He pulls out a document and stares at it intensely, as if to read the words again. He places the document on top of the file.

(*Under his breath.*) Looks like another one-sided conversation today.

Silence.

So, (*pauses*) hmmm . . . the appeal for the stay of execution got rejected . . . again

Silence.

Won't you say something? Are you going to walk into the gallows without so much as a fight? A fight for your life?

A dry mirthless laughter bursts out from the dark. The laughter ends as abruptly as it has started.

Even if you feel you have lost all hope, what about your siblings? At least they count. Say something . . . If not for yourself but for your younger ones . . . Mercy and Moses.

Silence.

The government is taking them away. They will be separated and given to foster parents. Are you not concerned about that?

Miriam (*speaks in a dry bristle voice*)   Anywhere is better.

Lawyer (*shocked to hear her voice*)   What did you say?

Miriam   Anywhere is better than the hell from which they have come.

The sounds of chains clanging and movement in the dark. **Lawyer** *peers into the dark and from the dark side of the stage steps out* **Miriam**. *She moves to centre stage and stands under the single light bulb. Her hands and feet are bound together in chains. She has on a dark colour shapeless prison garb. Her young face is smeared with dirt and her eyes are dead and old. Her hair is a mess, rough and dirty.* **Lawyer** *is surprised to see her. He moves downstage right and turns in profile to* **Miriam**.

Lawyer (*surprised*)   You have found your voice?

Miriam (*speaking to the audience, oblivious of the lawyer*)   Anywhere is better than the hell from which we have come. I lived through it, watching, powerless to do anything.

Lawyer (*excited*)   Now that you have started talking, perhaps if we got your story out there, we could save your life . . . you never know . . . I could find a technicality to work with . . . Although time is not on our side. The people are pressing for an immediate execution . . . Once the governor signs . . . (*He makes for the pile of documents in the file and pulls out a pen.*)

Miriam*'s dry laughter interrupts* **Lawyer**.

Miriam (*turns to* **Lawyer**)   Death is not a threat. It is a consolation.

Lawyer   But why? Pray tell, why did you do that to your uncle? The man who provided shelter and food for you and your siblings after the death of your mother . . .

Miriam   The man who took and got more than he gave . . . he took three lives and I took one. Fair enough, I guess . . .

Lawyer   Fair? You murdered the only guardian you had left in the world, and now your siblings are desolate orphans. No family, no love, nothing! What was his offence that was so terrible? Did he touch you inappropriately? Abuse you? (*Pause.*) Rape? Even at that, you could have reported to the police or the elders, or anyone.

Miriam (*smiles wryly*)   I guess rape is not such big a crime. After all, he fed and provided for us. Is that what you are trying to say? (*She turns and stares at the audience.*) What's in a woman's body they say? What's so unique about it? If a man would possess it one day then any man can have it. Especially the one who is family and has fed and clothed you with his generosity. A poke every now and then can't do much harm, surely? All you have to do is to submit to the groping hands, lay supine, spread your legs, raise your skirt high, close your eyes, and in five minutes the nightmare will be over.

Lawyer (*his voice rising in anger*)   I am not trying to justify rape, I am just being practical here.

Miriam   Oh! Yes, you are. Just like the policeman who said, 'Are you not a big girl?' or the elder that said, 'It is not as if you are a virgin, is this your first time?' or the neighbours that said, 'He is a man, he needs this thing once in a while, there is nothing new about it.' Or the woman who said, 'You need to be more tolerant. Everyone has a secret.' (*Sneers.*) Surely, you have your own excuse to add to the long list of justifications.

Lawyer   Miriam, no matter how bad one has had it, you cannot justify taking the law into your hands.

Miriam   Even for a murderer?

Lawyer   Yes, even for that. Unless in self-defence. But the victim here has killed no one, at least none that we are aware of. If anything, you were the one who sent a man to his grave with a kitchen knife in the most brutal manner. Stabbing him over a hundred times and making mincemeat of his groin.

Miriam (*angrily*)   He raped, he plundered, he made desolate. He killed the body and the spirit. Death was too good for him. He deserves eternal damnation.

Lawyer   Look, Miriam, emotions won't save you from the hangman's noose. Your uncle, Chief Alamasaga, was a respected member of this community. A philanthropist, an astute businessman, a family man and an upright man. Generous to all. He was building an orphanage for the community, even after he had donated a school to the community and a two-bedroom bungalow to the local police chief. He gave scholarships and interest-free loans to many. It is a great loss to the community. The people are angry and demanding justice.

Miriam (*angrily*)   But he was also an abuser. A rapist and a paedophile. Nothing was sacred to him. Not the girl child nor the boy child. I would rather go to the depths of hell than watch him ruin another life as he ruined mine (*pause, speaks in a quieter voice under her breath*) and that of my siblings.

Lawyer, *shocked, grabs the table to steady himself. He slowly lowers himself into the iron chair. This time he is the one facing the audience.*

Lawyer (*aghast*)   He touched your younger ones? Mercy and Moses?

Miriam (*smirks*)   Not touched them, my dear legal counsel. He abused them . . . sexually molested them. It was not enough for him that he had ruined my life totally and beyond redemption. Five pregnancies in two years . . . all for him . . . my mother's brother. But when the juice of my youth had run dry for him, he turned to the next life to devour. My underaged siblings . . . five and eight years old . . .

Lawyer (*holds his head, aghast*)   No! No! No! This is too much. No one is going to believe it. Not now, not ever. How do I even know you are saying the truth? How do we prove that this is not the ranting of a lost mind? Coming from a place of desperation? Anything to escape death? Why now? Since this crime happened you have not spoken a word. Not even in court. Now, tell me this is not your imagination at play. (*He stands up and points at* **Miriam** *accusingly*.) You have had time to prepare a good story, right? All

the days you sat in the dark, silent, this was what you were
thinking of . . .

Miriam *laughs hysterically, then stops just as abruptly. Turns to
the audience, and stares intensely at them.*

Miriam   Not even my lawyer believes me. Do you believe me?

A dirge rises slowly from the orchestra.

Blackout.

The End.

Desperanza

Kaulana Williams

Kaulana Williams is a coloured performing artist and theatre maker from Cape Town, South Africa. She holds an MA in Theatre Studies from Stellenbosch University and a BA (Honours) in Drama from the University of Cape Town. Kaulana spent ten years teaching theatre arts in private arts schools and public schools. She has written plays, directed her own work, acted for film and stage, and has created and performed several performance art/live art pieces. Kaulana's practice has always been concerned with coloured identity within the specific historical and social context of the Cape; particularly from the lens of the woman. She has used her writing and performing to explore her own ancestry and the impact that history has had on her life and art. Kaulana's work explores themes of violence and trauma on the psyche and on the body; particularly as it manifests in South Africa's epidemic of gender-based violence. In 2021, she formed a femme-only writers' circle of women playwrights to encourage and help develop her fellow playwrights, as well as create an avenue to develop her own work further. Kaulana wrote and produced two plays that were staged at the National Arts Festival Fringe at Makhanda, *A Girl's Best Friend* and *Pocket Shots*. Her first play written in Kaaps was staged as a performed reading at the Artscape Theatre as part of the New Voices programme in 2019. It is called *The After Party* and was directed by Lee-Ann Van Rooi.

Synopsis

Desperanza finds three sisters in a moment of crisis. Youngest sister Maytie is going through a personal turmoil and confides in oldest sister and matriarch Uriel that she wants to end her own life. Unable to rush to her sister's aid because of her responsibilities as mother to three children, Uriel sends middle sister Joanna to stop Maytie before it's too late. But Maytie has a secret that she cannot share with Joanna. Not her. Not the childless Joanna who has been desperately trying to have a baby for ten years. On the doorstep of Maytie's flat, through the door, the sisters have the most difficult conversation of their lives. They struggle to understand one another, but Joanna stays and insists on keeping her sister talking, keeping her alive. As much as Maytie wishes it was Uriel on the other side of the door, she recognizes that Joanna loves her and is desperate for her to stay. So, they keep talking. They keep reaching out through the door to one another, desperate to maintain the connection. *Desperanza* challenges the notions and expectations of motherhood for women. It highlights the suffering of those who feel pressured to give birth, despite the physical limitations and risks thereof. The play further highlights the importance of a woman's right to family planning and how dramatically it can alter the trajectory of her life.

Characters

Maytie (Florence May) a bohemian free-spirit type coloured woman in her early twenties. She is an art teacher who teaches yoga and meditation as her side-hustle. Her life is very full of her work and her social group of friends and, while she comes from a very tight-knit family, she does not see much of her siblings.
(First played by Bernice Nuna Quashie)

Joanna a high-strung coloured woman in her late twenties. Joanna is Maytie's older sister and Uriel's younger sister. She fancies herself the matriarch of the three, though she is not. Joanna's whole existence is wrapped around her role as wife and mother. She has been trying unsuccessfully to conceive a child with her husband for ten years now. Her struggles with fertility are a silent cross that she bears without letting anyone know about them.
(First played by Ekua Ekumah)

Uriel *merely the voice on the phone*, Uriel is the oldest of the three sisters. She is an easy-going, light-hearted, and warm coloured woman in her late thirties. She sometimes struggles to understand her siblings due to the age gap, but she enjoys being needed and is the defacto 'Mr Fix-it' in her family. While she has her own children to take care of, she jumps at the chance to take care of her extended family. She is a busy working mum of three boys.
(First played by Maame Adwoa Amissah Quayson)

Setting

The set is divided in half to reveal the inside of Maytie's small granny flat and the yard area just outside its front door. Maytie lives in a one-bedroom granny flat in the backyard of a local family's home (the Van Den Bergs). She knows the family through her job at a primary school, but they give each other their space and privacy and don't interact unless necessary. There is a separate gate and path leading to the granny flat and the main house is out of sight and earshot. On Stage Right we can see part of the yard, a path leading up to the front door of the granny flat, a cafe-style table and chairs, and several potted plants in colourfully painted pots. On Stage Left we see a sparse but colourfully decorated lounge area. There is a couch and a comfortable chair, a coffee table and a kitchen counter indicating the kitchen area. There is no dining table. The room is cluttered with newspapers, magazines, books, clothing, art supplies and general clutter. There are indoor plants, but they are dying for lack of attention. (This is in direct contrast to the happy, healthy plants just outside.)

At the play's start, the lights are not fully up, but we can vaguely see Maytie scrambling around in the lounge. She is looking for something but seems to have forgotten what it is that she is looking for and then remembers as she goes. She is visibly upset and confused. She is completely distracted in her search and keeps stopping to fold a piece of clothing or spot a withering plant and look around for a watering can or smell a bowl of leftovers. She continues this as we hear the phone call.

Voice-over:

Ringing and then phone is picked up.

Joanna   Hello?

Uriel   Hey, girl. How's it going?

Joanna   Fine, hey. And you?

Uriel (*sighing deeply*)   Girl, it's not me. I'm okay. Actually, I'm not. I'm a mess. Is now a good time?

Joanna   Yeah. Yeah. Sorry, I couldn't take your call earlier. I was driving.

Uriel   Yeah. You said. Listen, when was the last time you spoke to Maytie?

Joanna   Maytie? Sjoe. I can't think . . . maybe Marcus's birthday? When was that? Last month?

Uriel   The month before. It's been two months.

Joanna   Of course! Of course. Yes, two months ago. I mean, she sent memes and I replied with a heart or a smiley face or so . . .

Uriel (*impatient*)   Yes. Uh-huh. Are you busy this evening? Like now. Are you busy now?

Joanna   Uh . . . I mean, I just got home. I need to pack out these groceries, fix Marcus's supper . . .

Uriel   There's an emergency with Maytie. I mean, I think Maytie's in trouble and I can't get there. Can you go? It's an emergency.

Joanna (*unsure*)   I don't know. I've really got a lot on, Uriel, I can't just up and leave like . . .

Uriel   I wouldn't ask if I could go and deal with it myself. (*Beat.*) Jo . . .

Joanna (*concerned*)   Yes . . .

Uriel (*starts to cry*)   I don't know, Jo . . . I don't know what's going on there with Maytie. But, she's not okay. She sent me a message like . . . like a suicide message, Jo! Like she was saying she's sorry and not to tell so-and-so and not to tell Mummy . . . It was just scary, Jo. Maytie's never sent a message like that before. Can you just go?

Joanna *runs onstage as the voice-over continues playing. She runs up to the front door. She's about to knock, but stops herself. She seems to be trying to convince herself to proceed. She knocks. There is no answer. She paces in the yard. She knocks again.*

Uriel (*continuing*)   I tried phoning her right back! I sent how-many messages. It's like her phone's turned off! Nothing is going through. She's not answering. If I could get in my car and go, I would've been there already. But, it's just mad here! Keegan's at practice till late, I must fetch Kurt by the library now, I don't know what time Byron's coming home . . .

Joanna   Okay, I hear you. Okay. Don't worry about it. I'll go.

Uriel (*sobbing*)   Thank God! Thank you, Jo. Just hurry and get there before she does something to herself. Please! Let me know as soon as you know anything. I'll come as soon as I can!

Joanna   Don't worry about it, Uriel. I'll take care of it. She'll be fine. I promise. Bye.

Uriel   Thank you. Bye.

The phone clicks off.

Lights come up on **Joanna** *waiting at the front door and* **Maytie** *looking for something inside. She is dishevelled and has been crying.* **Joanna** *knocks at the door again.*

Joanna   Maytie! Hello? I know you're in there, sis, I can hear you! (*She looks through the front window and sees* **Maytie** *with her back to her.*) Ah! Exactly! I can see you too! Open the door!

Maytie (*hearing a far-off voice*)   Hello?

Joanna (*knocking*)   Hello! Florence May! Open the flipping door, man!

Maytie *realizes that there is someone at the door. She goes to open it, but stops herself realizing that it could be her imagination or some stranger.*

Maytie   Who is it?

Joanna   Not funny, Maytie! You've got us worried sick here! (*In a sing-song voice.*) It's your flipping sister, Joanna!

Maytie (*confused*)   Were we doing something today?

Joanna   No. (*Calming down*) No, no plans. I just came to see how you were.

Maytie (*confused*)   I'm fine.

Beat. **Joanna** *looks around confused. She is unsure of how to proceed.*

Joanna   Uhm . . . Okay then. Can I come in?

Maytie (*suspicious*)   Did you come alone?

Joanna (*realizing* **Maytie** *is being evasive*)   Uhm . . . yah. Can't I come alone?

Maytie   So you just came alone without phoning to . . . hang out?

Joanna   I did phone. Your phone is off. Uriel's been trying to phone too. I just wanted to see how you were.

Maytie   Did Uriel send you?

Joanna (*suspicious*)   No . . . she just mentioned she couldn't get hold of you.

Maytie   Is she also gonna just stop by?

Joanna (*frustrated*)   What is this now, Maytie?! Since when do you not let your sisters just stop by! *Jislaaik*! I was in the area and thought let me just stop by and see how my sissy's doing! We never hear from you, you're always so busy!

Maytie (*distracted*)   I have been very busy . . .

Joanna   . . . (*Listens for more, but* **Maytie** *is finished.*) Are you busy now? Is now a bad time?

Beat. **Maytie** *fidgets, unable to find a suitable answer.* **Joanna**
listens through the door, unable to discern what **Maytie** *is doing.*

Joanna   Uhm . . . maybe if . . . maybe if I can just use your toilet?
Then I'll be on my way?

Maytie (*confused*)   No . . . no, that's not what's going on here.
Why are you really here?

Joanna *paces the yard, unsure of whether she should reveal the
truth to* **Maytie** *or not. She negotiates with herself, rehearsing
what she's going to say.* **Maytie** *leans up against the door,
straining to hear what she is doing out there.*

Joanna   So . . . so, you sent Uriel a message. Do you remember
that? (*Beat.*) Do you remember what you said in the message?

Silence. **Maytie** *knows exactly what she's talking about and tries to
hold back tears.* **Joanna** *strains to hear what* **Maytie** *might be
doing on the other side of the door.*

Maytie (*quietly*)   Are the Van Den Bergs there?

Joanna (*looking offstage towards the main house*)   If they are,
there's not a peep out of them. They're probably worried about
their own business . . . they're not worried about our things . . .
Maytie?

Beat. **Maytie** *is struggling to hold back the tears and seem normal
in her responses. She doesn't want* **Joanna** *to suspect how
desperate she is.*

Maytie (*quietly*)   I'm here.

Joanna (*going right up to the door, quietly*)   So, the message?
Why did you send Uriel that message, sis?

Maytie   I . . . I don't know. I just felt really low, I guess.

Joanna   Well, you reached out, and that's good. Now I'm here,
sis. Tell me about it. (*She takes a chair and sits up against the
door.*) You may be low, but you're not rock-bottom, so now tell me
about it.

Maytie (*sits down up against the door*)   You wouldn't understand.

Joanna   Try me. I might surprise you. I've lived a lot longer than you. I've seen it all.

Maytie (*looking resentfully in her direction*)   You haven't seen this. (*Beat.*) And even if you have, it's not something I can talk about to you.

Silence as **Joanna** *tries to find the words to say next.* **Maytie** *is fighting confusing feelings of anger, sadness, desperation.* **Joanna** *fidgets with her handbag. She takes out her phone. She is unsure if she should call* **Uriel**. *She tries to text. She doesn't know what to say. She puts the phone back in the handbag.*

Joanna   So, what? You killed an old granny in the supermarket checkout line?!

Maytie (*laughing in spite of her feelings*)   What?! No! What would I even kill her with? A baguette?!

Joanna (*relieved to hear her laugh*)   Maybe, I don't know. But, knowing you, it would have to be gluten free!

Maytie (*wiping tears from her face with her sleeve*)   I don't know. Wouldn't that be a waste of a perfectly good loaf?

Joanna   You see? There's nothing so bad in the world. Whatever is happening, there is a way out. Whatever you did, there are loads of people doing worse all over the world. Whatever was done to you, you have more than enough re-enforcements to get them back. Or, what's the point in having sisters?

Silence. **Maytie** *seems to feel encouraged, but then bursts into tears. Hearing this,* **Joanna** *is concerned once again.*

Joanna   Please, sis. Just talk to me. I won't come in. I'll sit right here. Just tell me something. Some small part of it.

Maytie   I know why you and Marcus never had kids.

Silence. **Joanna** *is shocked. This has caught her completely off guard.*

Maytie   It's just . . . I know how badly you want kids. I don't want them, but . . . it's different for you.

Joanna (*pretending to laugh, while wiping tears from her face with her sleeve*)   Ha! Why are we talking about me now? We're supposed to be talking about you! About what's got you so low that you're sending scary messages, sis.

Maytie   I'm sorry. I didn't mean to scare anybody.

Joanna   It's fine! It's fine! But, you obviously sent it for a reason. Because things weren't at that point yet, because . . .

Maytie   'At that point'? Do you mean suicide?

Joanna (*silently freaking out*)   Uhm . . . I'm not saying that's what you meant, but . . . I mean, . . . is that what you meant?

Maytie   Was I telling Uriel that I wanted to kill myself? No . . . (**Joanna** *perks up hopefully*.) I was telling Uriel that I was about to kill myself, and that I had a few messages to leave behind. For some people.

Joanna *is crushed. She starts to sob, but is desperately trying to hide this from* **Maytie***. At some point, she needs to get up and walk to the end of the path. She uses the gate to steady herself. She is having a massive silent meltdown in the yard. She paces like* **Maytie** *in the opening, distracted, distraught.* **Maytie** *sits still on the floor, leaning against the door. She is oblivious to* **Joanna***'s performance outside; she is lost in her own thoughts.*

Joanna (*sitting by the door*)   Were you . . . doing it when I got here?

Maytie (*looking down*)   Yes. Trying to.

Joanna   Oh, sissy! I'm so so sorry. (**Joanna** *buries her head in her hands.*)

Maytie   It's actually a lot of admin. They make it seem pretty simple in novels.

Joanna   But why, sissy? Why? (*Beat.*) I mean, I've already interrupted you, you might as well tell me?

Maytie (*resentfully*)   It doesn't really matter. (**Joanna** *is about to say something when* **Maytie** *interrupts her.*) And, anyway, if I tell you, you're going to hate me forever. That's not how I want you to remember me.

Joanna   No. No one wants to be remembered poorly. (*Beat.*) But, I'm anyways here? You can write it on a page and slide it under the door?

Maytie (*panicking*)   I don't know. I don't know. (*Crying.*) I don't want to tell you, but I can't just do it while you're sitting there! And how will you know it's over? If I unlock the door, you'll just come in and stop me. But, if I leave it locked you'll have to kick it in and, knowing you, you'll probably twist your ankle trying to break the door down!

Joanna (*having to shout over her*)   Okay! Okay! The Van Den Bergs have a key! (**Maytie** *stops shouting.*) I can just get the key from the Van Den Bergs when . . . when you're done. (**Maytie** *sits back down by the door.*) But, I'm hoping you change your mind, sissy. I really really need you to change your mind.

Joanna *starts to sob. She stands facing the door, almost trying to look through it to get a glimpse of her sister.* **Maytie** *also cries softly.*

Maytie (*quietly*)   I didn't wanna have a baby, sissy. I was pregnant. I didn't want to do it.

Joanna (*suddenly hyper-alert*)   You were pregnant? (*Beat.*) And now?

Maytie   I went for an abortion. But, they couldn't do it. My heart. It wasn't safe. (*Beat.*) I don't want to do it, Jo! I just don't want to have to do it!

She sobs uncontrollably on the floor. **Joanna** *tries desperately to wrap her head around what she's been told. She can't find the words. She is in total shock.*

Joanna   But . . . but, how?

Maytie (*sitting up*)   There was that forest retreat. There was a guy. One of the facilitators.

Joanna (*still dazed*)   He forced himself on you?!

Maytie   No! No. It was great. We had a deep connection, you know? I don't understand it! It doesn't make any sense. I'm on birth control!

Joanna   Okay, but things happen. Sometimes . . . you try everything, but then God has other plans . . .

Maytie (*standing up*)   Do you think God has anything to do with this?! Seriously?! With denying you, who's desperate, a baby, but then forcing me who doesn't want anything to do with one to carry it to term!

Joanna (*reality dawns on her*)   So, your plan was to kill yourself because they won't give you an abortion?!

Maytie (*shouting across the door*)   Obviously! What did you think I was talking about?!

Joanna (*flabbergasted, shouting back*)   Not that! What the hell, Maytie?!

Maytie   Oh, I'm sorry you're feeling all let down! But I did say that if I told you, you would hate me forever!

Joanna   I don't hate you! My God! I just don't understand! Your whole life you'll throw down the toilet because you have to have a baby?! It's mad, Maytie!

Maytie   Oh? Oh? I'm mad! Great. Excellent. You're telling the suicidal person they're mad!

Joanna (*backing down*)   No. No, I mean . . . (*Suddenly angry again.*) Yes! You're crazy. You can just pop the baby out and move on with your life! Put it up for adoption, hell, Marcus and I will take it off your hands! But, to kill yourself?!

Maytie (*spelling it out slowly*)   Because I don't want to be pregnant!

Joanna   It's not even a year of your life. How far along are you? The school will give you maternity leave. You can do all that yoga stuff and your body will be back looking like you were never pregnant!

Maytie   But, I'll be lactating. The 'snap back' body is a myth! I'm a yoga instructor for dozens of women trying to get it right. I know!

Joanna *realizes the screaming match is not helping. She moves to sit by the door again. She moves the chair out of the way and sits on the floor like* **Maytie**, *leaning up against the door.*

Joanna   Maytie. Please. I know this is a major disaster for you. I do understand. I hear you. I just don't want to lose my little sister today, you know? Maybe we can go see a specialist? Maybe a second opinion? Maybe, medically speaking, there's another way? (**Maytie** *sits back down.*) Please, sissy. Please! Forget about me and my issues getting pregnant. This isn't about me. Uriel and I, Mummy and all of us, we'll do anything to keep you around. Sissy. Please?

Maytie   I don't know what to do, Jo. I'm just so tired. I feel like I've been crying over this for weeks. For years. (*Begins to sob.*) I don't even know how long it's been. I don't know what day it is. It's all just a mess, Joanna. My life is a mess. I don't even know myself anymore.

Joanna *tries to hug her through the door.* **Maytie** *sobs. We hear a car pulling up; the engine is turned off and someone gets out of a car door.* **Joanna** *looks towards it and sits back against the door, exhausted. The two sisters are now sitting back-to-back.*

Joanna   Oh, it's Uriel.

Maytie   Goddammit.

Lights fade to black.

The End.

Glossary

Jislaaik – Nice
Sjoe – Shoo
Coloured – self-defining term used for people of mixed-race heritage
     in South Africa

Oh!

Miliswa Mbandazayo

Miliswa Mbandazayo is an actress and writer based in Cape Town, South Africa. She graduated with a theatre degree from the University of Cape Town in 2021. Her interests are in adapting ancient literary texts for contemporary audiences and writing about the Black woman's perspective of the African contemporary experience. As a creator she has a variety of skills that range from performing, writing and dramaturgy. When she isn't working as an actress, she spends her time working on various writing projects, both personal and collaborative. Most recently she has been working as a scriptwriting and production mentor for the Baxter Theatre Centre's Zabalaza Festival since 2021.

Synopsis

Sakhe and Linda are a happily married couple, with what they both know to be a steamy sex life. When Sakhe goes away, Linda learns to play . . . revealing a truth about herself and her relationship with Sakhe. Will Sakhe play too? Or is this the end for this loving couple?

Characters

Linda, *a thirty-three-year-old Black South African working-class woman* (first played by Elsie Catherine Amoah)

Sakhe Sakhesizwe, *Linda's husband, a thirty-five-year-old working-class man* (first played by Joseph Kobina Hagan)

Setting

Bedroom

Linda *and* **Sakhe**'*s bedroom.* **Linda***, dressed in a gown and nightdress, is on the phone.*

Linda   I know. Well, I mean now I know . . . I don't know. (*Pause.*) Of course not! (*Pause.*) Yes, I'm going to tell him, but at the right time. In the right way . . . (*Pause.*) Yes, I'm going to do it before it happens again . . . (*Pause.*) I know that. (*Pause.*) Fine. What's good for me is better for him and great for us. (*Pause.*) Yes I'll use it. (*Pause.*) Okay. Thank you for . . . you know.

Sakhe *walks in and begins to undress . . . Moving towards his wife.*

Linda (*still on the phone*)   I think the red one looks best on you. (*Pause.*) Trust me – you're going to look great in that meeting. (*Pause.*) Okay, love you, bye. (*To* **Sakhe**.) Someone misses me . . .

Sakhe   Always. Did you miss me?

Linda   You know I did. I hate when you leave for so long

Sakhe   I know . . .

They kiss and make out.

Linda   Baby . . .

Sakhe   Hmmmm

Linda   I want us to try something . . .

Sakhe   What do you want me to do to you? Or is there something you want to do to me . . . oh I'm liking this.

Linda *gets up nervously and retrieves an object where she has been hiding it.*

Linda   Just hang on

Sakhe   What is it? What are you hiding? Come on, baby. I don't want to wait.

Linda (*she shows him the object*)   I want you to use this on me . . .

Sakhe   What is it? Is this one of those massage things? (*Taking the object, inspecting it.*)

Linda   Seriously? No it's a –

Sakhe   I'll do it later. Come on, baby. (*Tossing the object.*)

Linda   No. Wait. Just slow down. It's a vibrator and I want us to use it. I want you to use it on me.

Sakhe   What?

Linda   A vibrator. I want you to . . .

Sakhe   I heard you. (*Inspecting it.*)

Silence.

Linda   Well? You want to try? It'll be fun, I promise.

Sakhe   Now? You want to . . . with this?

Linda   Yes, I used it when you were away . . . when I was missing you. I've had it for a few months but hadn't really felt I needed to until a few days ago . . . when you weren't here.

Sakhe   And you feel the need to use it now? With me?

Linda   No, baby. I mean, yes I want to –

Sakhe   What are you saying? Why do we need this? You just said you didn't need it until I was away. I'm here now, baby. Come on . . . You're wasting time. Didn't you say you missed me? Clearly you did if you've been fiddling with this . . .

Linda   I did miss you. But just wait, Sakhe. I really think we can . . . we will both enjoy this, trust me.

Sakhe   Okay maybe next time. Right now I just want . . .

Linda (*firmly*)   No.

Silence . . .

Sakhe   No?

Linda *shakes her head.*

Sakhe   Because of a vibrator when you have a real man in front of you –

Linda You're not . . .

Sakhe – a man who loves you, makes you feel good. Pleasures you immensely . . .

Linda *is quiet.*

Sakhe What?

Linda What do you mean?

Sakhe That look. Linda, what am I missing here?

Linda When you were away . . .

Sakhe Did you fuck someone?

Linda No, never. I used the . . . vibrator. But . . .

Sakhe Speak, baby. What is it?

Linda I used the vibrator for the first time. It felt really good. Then it felt amazing. I felt amazing . . . I experienced something beyond what I can describe.

Sakhe *is impatient.*

Linda I had an orgasm.

Sakhe Well, that makes sense. Great! We've established you got what you paid for. What has that got to do with us, right now?

Linda I had an orgasm. I had an orgasm for the first time in my life, Sakhe. I didn't . . .

Sakhe (*laughs loudly*) You're going to stand there after all these years and tell me nonsense. Ah! I know women fake but some things can't be faked. You telling me every time I made you cum you faked it. Please, Sisi.

Linda No. I don't know. Maybe . . . no I don't think so. I'm trying to make sense of this.

Sakhe Oh, you don't think so? How do you not know? I know. Oh, please.

Linda Sometimes. But there were times I thought . . . Until the other day. Then I realized.

Sakhe Realized what? What about when I? (*Gesture.*) And when I? (*Gesture.*) And when I do the thing with my . . .? (*Gesture.*) So what are you on about?

Linda I'm saying I had an orgasm for the first time in my thirty-three years. The best feeling. The best and yes only orgasm I've ever had apparently. I didn't know what happened was possible. But it is and I want to feel that with you. I want you to make me feel it. I want you to know how to make me feel like that. Get me there. I want you to want to. I want you to pleasure me like I pleasure you. Sakhe? Sakhe, I didn't know. What's good for me is better for you . . . Great for us.

Sakhe You're pissing me off.

Linda I didn't want you to react like this.

Sakhe Are you hearing yourself? Grown woman. You just told me our sex life has been a lie.

Linda No. But you also never asked me. Never asked how it really felt for me. Only that it was good. I didn't have a lot of . . . Look, now I know what I need. Time. It's important to me. It'll make me feel important, valued . . . loved. After some time I began to . . . That's all, just listen and slow down with me. For me.

Sakhe Linda. Linda. So now I'm bad in bed. Selfish. I'm not one of those guys and have never been. I am not selfish.

Linda Not what I said. I just want . . .

Sakhe Want? Let's talk about wants. Let's talk about your wants. How I meet every one of them. How that is what I was doing while you were having your little awakening with (*points at the vibrator*) . . . this. I'm selfish . . . but not selfish buying you this house. Not selfish buying your car. Not selfish giving you the lifestyle you wanted. I work damn hard for you. I give you everything. All of me! I was working damn hard for you the last two weeks. I come home, I miss my wife. I love my wife. I want to pour love on my wife that I've missed. Now you're telling me this bullshit. About listening and waiting or whatever. I listen and gave you all this . . .

Linda Don't do that, this a partnership. I'm just wanting to go deeper with you and give you more of me. It means slowing down and giving me more time. This is how we can be better. I discovered this and I want to experience it together.

Sakhe Yes, great for us. You said. After all I do. In here, I must labour, 'after some time', what the fuck? It's not like it doesn't feel good for both of us. I do more than most guys, you know.

Linda I wouldn't know . . . and it shouldn't matter.

Sakhe Right

Linda I love our life and all you do for us, what we do for each other. I just think –

Sakhe Then show me you know how to make me cum . . . (*He gestures provocatively.*)

Linda (*after a beat, angrily*) What? Sakhe, I –

Sakhe Fine, I'm tired now. I have to work in the morning. (*He dresses.*)

Linda Sakhe . . . Sakhe . . .!

Sakhe Good night.

He gets into the bed. **Linda** *looks at the vibrator quietly, places it back in the hiding place and gets into bed with her husband. Lights fade.*

The End.

In Her Silence

Faustina Brew

Faustina Brew is Senior Lecturer at the Department of Theatre Arts, University of Education, Winneba, Ghana. She obtained her PhD in Performance Practice (Drama) from the University of Exeter, UK, in 2016. Prior to this, she had obtained a Master of Fine Arts (Playwriting) degree from the University of Ghana, Legon, in 2006. She has published four stage plays: *Murder of the Surgical Bone*, *The Hot Chair*, *The Prisoner* and *The Birth of the Mystery Child*. Her articles published in refereed journals focus on practising process drama in unfavourable environments and the playwright's craft. Faustina has participated in several international conferences of professional associations, including the International Federation for Theatre Research (IFTR) African Theatre Association AfTA, International Theatre for Young Audiences Research Network (ITYARN) and International Association of Theatre for Children and Young People (ASSITEJ), as well as other academic forums. She has also directed several stage productions including stage adaptations of *Animal Farm*, *Romeo and Juliet* and *The Trials of Brother Jero* and *Jero's Metamorphosis* staged as a double bill. Currently, she teaches Playwriting and Drama in Education at the Department of Theatre Arts at both undergraduate and postgraduate levels. Her research interest includes playbuilding with children, interplay between child's play and learning, impact of theatre experiences on audiences and developing thought-provoking stage plays.

Synopsis

Can a woman 'say no' to sexual abuse perpetrated by her husband? John tries various means to get Ella (his wife), who has positioned herself outside the house, to move in because, as indicated by Ella, his sexual desire is at its peak. He tries several strategies but Ella refuses to succumb to his overtures. She reminisces about her life with John and how he's often used her as a sex object. Ella's responses are projected in sync with her body language.

Characters

Ella, *a middle-aged-wife* (first played by Ernestina Anokye Agyekum/Kelvin Andre Swanzy Menlah

John, *Ella's husband* (first played by Augustine Enninful)

Settings

On the porch, living room

The scene takes place on the porch of the couple's house. **Ella** *is seated. Her dress is quite casual but elegant. Her demeanour shows she's unhappy. Throughout the play, she doesn't speak; her thoughts and responses are projected on a screen in sync with her actions.* **Ella**'s *long lines should be split on different slides to make reading easier for the audience.* **John** *enters from inside, observes* **Ella** *for a while and moves closer to her.*

John   Hi, sweetheart.

Ella   Is he referring to me?

John   My beauty, my love . . .

Ella   I know he's up to something.

John   Sweetheart, you know I love you. You are the only one in my life.

Ella   Will this man just get out of my sight?

John   I know you are angry with me, but you shouldn't take it this far. It was just a little misunderstanding.

Ella   You call that a little misunderstanding, right?

John   For more than two weeks, you've been like this. For how long is this going to continue?

Ella   I understand that better; it's been more than two weeks since he had his way with me.

John   Forgive me, sweetheart! I will make it up to you.

Ella   I know what you want, but it's not going to happen this time.

John   Give me a little smile. I know you love me.

Ella   Idiot, my stupidity has expired.

John   Sweetheart, talk to me. Your silence is too loud.

Ella   I've been silent for close to three weeks now. Has he just noticed it?

John   Darling, I'm thinking we should take a holiday, go somewhere nice and have fun.

Ella   Now, this is getting annoying. Will someone tell this idiot to leave me alone!

John (*holds* **Ella**)   Sweetheart, I love you.

Ella   Hush, you are suffocating me. Can you stop this?

John *is all over* **Ella** *now.*

Ella   Something should interrupt this man, a phone call or something.

John (*loosens his grip on her*)   Ella, can we go in? We need to talk.

Ella   I look like a fool to you, right?

John   I am never going to hurt your feelings again, I promise.

Ella   It's always been this way. When you want sex, you become the best of a husband. As soon as you get what you want, we are back on the battlefield until another two weeks when your sexual desire peaks again.

John   Ella, you know I love you, don't you?

Ella   Yes, seasonal . . . when you want sex.

John *exits.*

Ella   Such a relief. He shouldn't come back here. How I wish I could seek divorce. Only if our society doesn't frown on such action.

John *returns.*

Ella   Oh, my God, he's back.

John   Sweetheart, I got something for you. It's not a lot, but it's quite substantial. Buy anything you want.

Ella   What! What does he take me for? A lady of the night? Where is this demeaning idea coming from?

John (*getting frustrated as* **Ella** *refuses to take the money*)   How long are you going to stay outside? Come in; mosquitoes will soon feast on you.

Ella   I prefer to stay with the mosquitoes. They don't have any intentions of causing harm; they only want food.

John   I've seen that you've served my food. I'm grateful but . . . why can't we eat together?

Ella   I'm not hungry.

John   Ella, don't do this to me. I agree we've had challenges in our relationship, but you can't also deny the fact that we've had good times together.

Ella   When it pleases you.

John   Ella, Ella, please look at me.

Ella   He's remembered his old trick. This time you have failed. I'm no longer the fool.

John   You are frustrating me, Ella. Why are you becoming this difficult? Why? I'm your husband.

Ella   Even the high priest knows that.

John   Give me some respect, at least.

Ella   Have I done anything disrespectful?

John   I have been talking since I got home, over thirty minutes now, and you haven't said even a word, only making some faces. What's all this?

Ella   Frustration is setting in; that's good. He will soon leave me alone.

John   Bible says a wife should be submissive to her husband, at least obey God's command.

Ella   I guess 'love your wife' in the Bible is an error.

John   Okay, eat your pride. (*He exits.*)

Ella   It looks like I've won the battle this time. Wow! For the first time. I've suffered. I've become like an object to be used and dumped. Picked again as and when . . . But I must go in for sure. Won't he force himself on me again? He's always had his way. If only I could find a hiding place . . .

John *returns.*

John   Ella, the food is cold. Can you just get in and warm it for me?

Ella   You know how to operate the microwave, just heat the food yourself.

John   You don't even care about my food.

Ella   Not just your food, everything else, just leave me alone.

John   You can't stay out here forever; I'm going to wait for you inside.

Ella   Where can I have refuge? I have irritated him a lot; he's going to be rough with me. I must get out of here. But where to?

John   Ella, will you get in.

Ella   Oh no!

John   I don't want to force you; I don't want to be violent. Will you get in?

Ella   Dare touch me.

John   Wait, I will be back. (*Dashes in.*)

Ella   You can do your worst, and I will not submit this time. No! You can kill me. (**Ella***'s phone rings. She checks.*) Why is he calling me on my phone? Another strategy: it has failed completely.

John *peeps to check if she has picked up his call. She puts the phone down.*

John (*aside*)   What's gone so wrong this time? Maybe she's seeing someone. No, Ella can't do that no, she can't. So, what can it be? I've tried all the tricks I've used in the past . . .

Thinking, **John** *scrolls on his phone. Moves closer to* **Ella** *and plays 'Please Forgive Me' by Bryan Adams – just the chorus that says, 'Please forgive me'.*

Ella   What! What's he up to? It's a lie. He's not sorry for anything. I know what he wants.

John (*stops the music and smiles at* **Ella**)   You have forgiven me, haven't you? Let's go in.

Ella   I don't know what to do now. But one thing for sure, I'm not going in there. I won't be defeated.

John   Please, let's go in, I will make it up to you.

Ella   That will not happen. He will just force himself on me . . . and the pain . . . he won't even bother . . . he will get what he wants . . . and just say 'that was nice'. Then I groan in silence as I treat my wounds.

John   Ella, what's the matter with you? What's eating you up? Should I get a psychologist or maybe a psychiatrist? This is not normal.

Ella   Yes, I'm mad.

John   You are going in with me. (*Attempts to carry her.*)

Ella *manages to free herself and runs out.*

John   Ella, where are you going? Come back, come back, I say. (**Ella** *is out of sight now.*) She walks out on me . . . and gone away together with all the plans for tonight. I will get her. She must perform her duty. (*Runs out in same direction.*)

The End.

Horny & ...

Philisiwe Twijnstra

Philisiwe Twijnstra is an international award-winning South African playwright who works as a scriptwriting lecturer at the Durban University of Technology. She has an MA in Creative Writing from Rhodes University. Philisiwe was longlisted by Short Story Day Africa (2021) for her short story 'The Girl Named Uku/pha/za/mi/se/ka', published in 2021. Her award-winning play *The Road* and *The Blue Blue* toured and was produced by Swedish company Darling Desperados. Her short story 'Little Black Sandals' was produced by Talisman Theatre in Kenilworth, UK, for their YouTube series (2021). She received the CASA award for a residency to write her new play *Not Enough Buses in Spring* as well as receiving a fellowship in Germany in 2018. Her play *The Red Suitcase* was produced as a staged reading in Canada by Zee Zee Theatre Company (2018). Currently, she is writing a novel, *Sleeping Gods*.

Synopsis

Horny & ... is the story of a young woman recollecting her memories of pleasure, sensuality, vulnerability and sexual liberation for a Black female body. She is alone in a white room where a session of memory takes over whenever a certain sound comes up, which takes away doubt and censorship, allowing her to recollect without fear of retribution. This is her truth. She has volunteered for this new test of technology that helps a female body live and speak its truth – to remember what she has forgotten so that she can start the process of healing her anxieties – but she is the first woman to volunteer. No one knows the extent of these tests, and with each memory she gets lost, swallowed, dragged deeper into it. The question remains: will she find darkness or liberation?

Characters

Milakakuhle (Milla), *a thirty-two-year-old woman, wears a black tracksuit* (first played by Ekua Ekumah/Maame Adwoa Amissah Quayson)

Setting

On a set. The stage is divided into sections with cameras, and at centre stage there is a dressing table, with lamps suspended above her and surrounded by different types of chairs from benches, sofas and kids' plastic chairs to beer crates. Every chair is used to tell Milla's story. Some of the chairs have more furniture next to them, a bookshelf, a kitchen unit, and a table and lamp.

Scene One

Milla *sits at a dressing table, with a mirror attached, and a dangling red lamp is suspended above centre stage. She looked shrivelled. She is looking at herself in the mirror, touching her body guided by heaviness and reluctance. She takes a deep breath, looks at the camera and her face is reflected on the big screen.*

Milla   Before we start, may I please have some water? Yeah! Thanks . . . Yes, I'm okay I just saw someone at the airport . . . yeah, yeah, unexpectedly. (*Pause.*) I'm good to begin.

Pause. She laughs.

I just wish I agreed to take the bus on my way here, maybe certain things would have been avoided. No, I don't mean about the ticket problem. I just said I met someone at the airport.

You know on the flight they said there was no space for luggage, we carry luggage isn't?

Water arrives and she quickly drinks. Makes a sound that is considered unladylike by society.

I have inherited my mother's pain. Her wounds and her trauma. And I have perfected them, in such a way that the only strength I have left in me is what my mother knew about her mum, to know where it all began and damn . . . honestly, I don't want my daughter to carry it forward.

Ayime la! *Ayigcine la . . . Ayibe no wo*! (It must stop here.)

Silence.

I have trouble remembering moments, this includes quite great moments in my life, but it is fine when you cannot remember how the hurt happened . . . in fact, I urge that to happen, forgetfulness is the solution to long-time trauma.

Long pause.

I wish to forget.

Silence, fixes her bra straps, inhales and looks at the camera as it zooms out her face.

But when the memory of pleasure is no longer there . . . it makes me wonder where my grave is.

Like the song 'Misty Blue' by Etta James . . . that song is a cry, a weep on my soul . . . from feeling absolutely everything to feeling nothing at all. What a shame! I'd rather feel the feeling of not feeling because it is terribly lonely to see the door being slammed continuously in your face.

I knock, I bang, I scream and shout . . . for the door to be unlocked . . . because there is terrible gloom and misery between my thighs, and the moment of knocking it's me a Black woman hoping that when the door opens, rain, lightning and storm will pour.

Pause. She unpacks pleasure toys under the tables, her face zooms on screen, captured by the camera.

It is a shame to detour from nature, a shame for this body to be discarded, from what it needs to do. It cannot be.

Smears herself with lotion.

The patch of sunlight passes by but a shadow from nowhere and with such obsession takes over. Just to find out that it's just there to discard you . . . like an old dull song. I feel like my body is forsaking me, by selecting which memory to hold on to. From the bottom of the hole that is where you see the damn light, trust a woman with hair shaved every four days to say that. Do you know what my body tells me, especially when I'm alone and when the dog is locked outside?

She laughs loudly and combines sexual moaning sound and laughter.

My mouth is dry, and my toes are never tingly.

Grabs more water.

Shame such days are not meant for brown bodies. (*Whispers to self.*) I'm a bull in a calf's skin, a mind not so unleashed, but I'm a walking museum, an archive of memories.

She undresses herself, clips off the bra and throws it on the floor.
Takes out the spandex throws it on the floor and puts on her gown.
Opens her legs wide.

Vala bo! *Vala bo* . . . close them legs they say, pluck them brows
they say . . . bio-oil them stretch marks they say. Mind you these
people never bought even a pantyliner for me.

Makes the unpleasant sound again.

Have you ever asked yourself why has God created a woman – just
think about it, what is God hiding? Come on, you must have asked
yourself questions. Because I do.

Fondles her breasts, stands and shouts a slogan.

NO BRA! LET THEM DANGLE! JINGLE! NO BRA!

Looks directly at the camera.

That should be illegal, right, a gravitational force drags everything
to the south.

'*Milakakuhle kumele umazi USIMAKADE*!' That was drilled into
me, like hardened cement drilled to the ground. My name is
Milakakuhle Zikode, horny and . . .

If there is more of me, then why do I feel so alone with empty
mirrors and a swelling, mounting clit? Yes, it's quite shocking to
hear that word . . . clit! Clit! Clit, clitoris . . . (*Pause.*) Crazy how I
was conditioned to fear the best and most fantastic parts of myself.
(*Puffs.*)

My God, do you know how layered my vulva is? Just the other day
I was talking to a friend of mine. I said to her, I saw it dangling out
of my thighs like a blanket trapped in the wind.

(*Make the sound of the wind.*) As soon as I wear my panty they
snatch back inside. As soon as I go to pee or whatever they dangle
and greet the air all over again . . . And this *vulvarian* nation down
there is beautifully layered, and I feel like I never took a chance to
know it. You know how frustrating it is that we never look down
there, we were told that it smells, and don't forget to close *them*

legs. Come on, my vagina is its own washing machine, baby . . . it does its own laundry. It is self-service.

Pause.

The weirdest and funniest and craziest thing ever is that *amakholwa* are everywhere. The first thing I was taught to love was God, know God and fear God because he was everywhere like a stranger that knows you and your ways. A part of me was not sure I wanted anyone to know me like that, it felt somewhat unfair because it took a moment away from me, to know myself. It was like preparing to live as a girl child was like preparing for battle, and the same God is seated on my chest reminding me to be an obedient home keeper.

She opens the cupboards, pours a bottle of whisky and gulps it up.

This whisky was in my grandmother's house where I grew up, had my first pains – do you know what pains I'm talking about? (*Pause.*) Periods. Aunty Sue. Red Dot. Real community causing havoc in my womb. We could not buy panadas because this pain was not really pain, right. It was just cramps. My grandmother pours her whisky and says drink. I do drink, but I wanted to have less pain. In the midmorning before leaving the house, I had to wash dishes, dry them, pack them then make a fire for cooking when I was done.

Scene Two

Milla Pray. Pray. Pray to be safe while playing outside with boys and pray that boys do not see my underwear. Pray that my breasts do not sprout like ripe peaches ready to be pulled one by one.

I was ripe. (*Laugh.*) I was eleven years old. My first boyfriend was Joseph – he had curly hair, and he didn't speak much but he silently taught me many things about my body. I leaned in, and he waited, and sometimes that is just what it took, for him to be patiently waiting for me. '*Milakakuhle.* Time to pray.' My grandmother had an angry voice, that shouted to God as if he was deaf. '*Geza izitsha*', she said.

Then they brought the small TV in the kitchen, I quickly wiped the table and slowly dried the dishes because I wanted to also watch *Generations*.[1] But I was not allowed because I was young. When everyone had left for their sleeping rooms, I was alone in the sponge. Usually in these hours, I believe the world was mine alone, moved just the way I liked it.

Spotlight comes up. From her pocket **Milla** *takes out a* doek *and ties it on her. She repeats this until she cannot tie any more, and now she looks like she is wearing a turban made from* doek.

The world asks so much of us to be mothers, caregivers, best friends, aunts and mentors. This flood of roles makes me a woman but the other side of me is unknown, some things I don't know how to navigate. I'm expected to make a house a home, but all my life a house has been the thing that made sense to me. I never wanted to be a mother, but society said that is my purpose, never wanted to marry but strong feelings manipulated certain translations.

Silence.

(*Looks at the audience.*) May you please dim the lights and maybe switch on some other ones when we can. (*Light changes.*) We – ? I'm confused by that. Sometimes at times I feel like I'm not alone, something takes over me. I reached a point not to ignore whatever it is that is intruding in this body since inception. (*Laughs.*) It is true I never asked to be here, a child never whispers to be born. I mean, if I knew this would have been my life, then good. This place is not my home, yet it is the only place I know. There is so much laughter from the moment one walks in, unexplained laughter, and when I look around no one flogs me here but, still, this place does not hold the weight of my name.

She stands then moves to two single beds and jumps on them. She feels like a kid. Almost like she gets lost in talking to someone. She laughs hysterically. Music plays loud, she dances to a crescendo and falls. In a zap the light changes into her spotlight.

---

1 *Generations*: long-standing South African television soap.

My twin died, and I made it out . . . lucky me, I guess. Sometimes I think I carry her sins as well. When I look around, I don't recognize whom I was meant to be. Between the police hippo and the promise of a Black man being released to grant us free days from a government that was infested with gangrene – there was me lying next to beer crates not remembering where my home was or which section I was in – was I at *Makhulong*? Or *popo*'s place?

Wherever I was the cement was cold.

I was sure about one thing though: the sound of Steve Kekana playing on the big hifi followed by beer crates being shifted, pulled and dragged.

I know what that meant; it was morning and *isikhathi sok'jola asekho, sokudangalezela obaba* no mama *ses'phephile*, and that also would mean that last night had gone by with nightmares and dreams. What excited me also was how I was missing the chance of finding coins because, believe me, mornings were high.

Aunty Mavis swept the ground like the beer queen shebeen she was.

Makes sweeping sounds.

Dust decides to move along with her in a very eager way because it goes quite quickly onto her face taking up her space – she flings her hand away, and it spreads. Aunty Mavis picks up *stompies* of cigarettes from the ground and dumps the remains from ash trays. Boyoyo Boys plays on the next track, Aunty Mavis pulls the broom to her chest and continues to dance. Every inch of her body moves with that broom. She even closes her eyes – now you know when that happens. Before she gets lost in it, she pulls the sofa, and then she sees me seeing her. We see each other and she puts one hand on her waist, and she says to me.

Shout. **Milla** *becomes the character of* **Aunty Mavis**.

Aunt Mavis   'Hey, *wena*, this is not your bed, *stek! Tsamaya, hamba.*'

Milla   I didn't move. 'I said *hamba, hamba bo. Ungazongijwayela kabi. Ucabanga ukuthi* this is a hotel. *Votsek mani Hamba!*'

She didn't have to be so loud – I was not deaf, not like *Umkhonto Ka Shaka*. Everyone knew that you had to call him ten times before he would respond. When you called him there was a chance he would not even recognize who he was speaking to, but I could hear, my ears *bezingenazo ingonogono*.

I lay on the ground, but I don't know why she had to repeat herself, it was not like I was like *Mkhonto Ka Shaka*, of course, I was planning on leaving, but my body was complaining on that cement I just had one too many to enable myself to walk at night. I could not walk at night because Sis Easter the lady I came with there left me with Bra Dube.

Tsenolong was another section and *Maokeng* was just another, like water there and paraffin there. I tried to stand but my feet clearly were not normal feet on the ground, they had other thoughts that belonged to the cracked feet. She helped me to stand and pushed me outside and there was Sis Esther in her peach ruffled dress, her bra straps – the bra hanging for dear life than the boobs . . . her bra straps were showing, and she came out of the room looking like she was at war with dogs and trucks.

Milla *becomes another character,* **Esther**.

Esther   'Ah there you are, Milla, *asambe*. Probably your grandmother is wondering where you are. Now, listen, don't tell things that happen in the night, okay, I mean your grandmother does not need that kind of stress. Okay.'

I nodded – what else was I to say? I knew if *gogo* knew that I had been in the shebeen and danced all night, and in between I might have slurred, forgotten my name, fallen on the ground. Whatever it was that may or may not have happened might have happened.

I had to go home; Sis Mavis had a job to do – she had to smooth talk her way out. But I'm saying this because I didn't know what my grandmother would say.

Silence.

Milla *becomes another character, a church woman testifying.*

'*Intombi, kumele izinze, ilinde, ngoba inkanuko ime emnyango, ngoba usathane ukhona, ulindile. Wena linda ume mi! Ume kuJehova!*'

Milla *back to herself. She looks at the camera, looks at the other one.*

Milla   How many volunteers are here?

Silence.

How many women are in this building? I'm remembering a lot – basically what you are doing to me is working. Or maybe it is not.

Pause.

There is something I'm not saying – isn't that why I'm here? (*Nods.*) I need a smoke.

Emotional, she pulls the camera closer to her face and looks at it for a long time. She stands and walks downstage to pick up water and drinks. After that she screams.

It is my truth to keep, I always said but the truth of truth is . . . I didn't hear myself saying it. I'm constantly at war with myself, trying to un-measure my own failed experiences. Frequently I go back to my past and try to rectify every wrong deed that was done to me. I pull every thread to make it fit the new needle that has fallen into my lap. I announced to the world that I was once a victim. The world expects me to live by its laws and continuously needs to be fed new meanings of what it meant being an angry, Black, bruised woman.

I looked at my daughter and I realized she knew none of these definitions or stigmas, she decided what she wanted to wear and do. I could only smile and looked at how free she was to think what she wanted without me imposing my own beliefs and norms on her.

One afternoon we were at home and my child said:

Milla *becomes the child.*

'I wanted to play soccer, Mama.'

One morning we were at the salon, and the hairstylist said:

Milla *becomes the hair stylist.*

'So many scratches, a girl must take care of their skin.'

Milla *becomes herself.*

And today here I stand, looking into the camera and I say: Some introductions are like beauty floating, but for women like me, it is like being trapped in a corner with sharp needles pinching holes in my body. Some introductions have the power to shape the ghosts hidden in our bones. My name is *Milakakuhle*, and these are my introductions.

(*Introduction one.*) I was six years old. A neighbour. Wearing his matching suit and tie. He had a ciggie in his fingers. I wore a flowery red dress. My grandmother had sent me to buy Coca-Cola. On my way to the shops, I saw him in his usual spot. I ended up in his house. He followed me behind and closed the door when he entered. Next thing he was licking his fingers to page through a magazine.

A magazine filled with people who preferred clothes on the floor, not on them. He asked me whether I wanted big breasts. I knew I wanted breasts because often my friends from three houses down from mine would put egg cardboard inside our flat chests and parade around the streets like older women. Like a nail being hammered on the ground, a hole gaped. Blood trickled down my inner thigh.

He stood up and left and sat under the tree. He pulled grapes from the grape tree and ate them and tucked his shirt inside his pants. I left with one Rand in my hand, trying to find a painless way to feel.

(*Introduction two.*) It was my first sleepover. During the day the woman in the house was a tyrant. She shouted at everyone for leaving breadcrumbs on the table, for leaving unmade blankets on the sponge mattress, for forgetting to empty a bucket of wee. But at night when dreams were underscored by sounds of snoring and tosses. I found her on top of me, playing house to house. She was a man, and I was a woman and the next day I was the man and she was the woman.

(*Introduction three.*) A woman of around twenty. I remember reminding her, saying you meant you have never slept with a woman. Feeling a little bit anxious myself because this was my first time with someone as beautiful as her. But she said no, she was a virgin. I was then reminded of what it was to be a virgin. Mine was non-existent when I was six. How does one become a virgin? I looked at her. She told me to handle her with ease because she was delicate. Where do I touch and not touch, and, most importantly, how do men break a virgin and live to tell the tale?

Pause.

(*Introduction four.*) A man, a woman, and in between them a young girl. My daughter ran towards me. My daughter was a spitting image of him. His eyes were wide open, his suitcase fell on the floor. He stood up slowly and walked towards me. I looked at him in his pilot's suit. Does he remember me when I was six? Does he remember me from Fourteen-six years ago?

Walk towards downstage. Light changes.

Six years old: raped. Twelve years old: pregnant. Twenty years old has an eight-year-old girl. At the airport, my eight-year-old meets her dad.

Lights fade.

The End.

Glossary

Vala bo! – Close them!
Kumele Umazi USIMAKADE! – You must know God/Almighty
Amakholwa – Christian believers
Amahosana Waya Waya – Hosanna everyday
Makhulong – The name of a place in Tembisa
Geza izitsha – Wash up
Doek – An Afrikaans word that means cloth. It is the traditional head covering used among most elderly or married women in rural areas

Isikhathi Sok'jola Asekho – There is no more time to date, to stretch our legs open for an older man. That time is gone

Sokudangalezela Obaba Ses'phephile – This is no longer time to be dating or opening wide our legs for older men . . . That time is gone

Stompies – Cigarette butts

Wena – You

Stek! – From *Votsek*, meaning go away

Tsamaya – SeSotho language, meaning go away

Hamba – IsiZulu language, meaning go away

Ungazongijwayela Kabi – Don't get used to me by disrespecting me

Ucabanga Ukuthi – Do you think that . . .

Votsek Mani – Go away, man

Umkhonto Ka Shaka – King Shaka's spear

Bezingenazo Ingonogono – This refers to someone's maturity – so they had no nipples

Mkhonto Ka Shaka – King Shaka's spear

Tsenolong – Name of a place in Tembisa

Maokeng – Name of a place in Tembisa

Asambe – IsiZulu language, meaning let's go

Gogo – IsiZulu language, meaning 'Grandmother'

Shebeen – A shebeen was originally a bar forbidden by law, where alcoholic beverages were sold without a licence

Intombi, kumele izinze, ilinde, ngoba inkanuko ime emnyango, ngoba usathane ukhona, ulindile. Wena linda ume mi! Ume kuJehova! – A young woman must be calm and wait, because lust is standing at the door, because the devil is there, waiting. You wait and wait, be still! Stand in Jehovah!

Gnash

Katlego K Kolanyane-Kesupile

Katlego K Kolanyane-Kesupile holds a sociology MA in Human Rights, Culture and Social Justice from Goldsmiths, University of London – specializing in disability theory, public space design, race and decoloniality; and a BA (Hons) in Dramatic Arts from University of the Witwatersrand – with specialities in design and directing. Beyond playwriting, her published literary work spans children's stories, fiction, academic texts and poetry. Along with being named one of the 100 Most Influential Women of African Descent by *OkayAfrica* in 2018, her accolades include being a TED Fellow, Chevening Scholar, International Women of Courage Award nominee and OutRight Action International UN Religion Fellow. When she's not seeking to craft a world where 'ignorance is a choice rather than an expected state', Katlego may be found singing, painting, cycling or lost in worlds of her own creation.

Synopsis

On the eve of the internationally sanctioned day of the purge – a zero consequence day established to manage the world's population when anyone can be prey or predator – in an unnamed part of the world, we meet two women each sent on an assassin's mission by the other. Frustration and uncertainty are interlaced with their murderous intentions, yet their friendship and faith promise to carry them beyond the new dawn. This dark comedy explores the bounds of love, loyalty and sociability.

Characters

Eunice, *fifty-two, moderate build, cornrows in a bun, has an air of polished kindness. Surprisingly mischievous* (first played by Tracy Himmans)

Paballo, *athletic build, wears a bob wig, a corporate professional air about her. Dry witted and a quick thinker* (first played by Araba Dansowaan Agyare)

Time

A future where an annual global purge has been agreed upon to manage mental health and population numbers.

Setting

A domestic kitchen in a middle-class home in the suburban outskirts of the city. This is the kind of house that has a garden in the back and lawn in the front. Three chairs sit at a chic, modern kitchen table off centre, right. The kitchen sink and kettle are implied on centre stage left, the stove is implied upstage right as well as the pantry. Upstage right of the pantry is the exit to the yard/laundry area.

Note to Set Designers: The colours in the room are muted pastels in earth tones and cool colours. Lighting may be used to bring the sub-aquatic feel to life, with moments of warmth and brightness.

On the table rests a pair of matching coffee mugs with football insignia, and an open newspaper with a sales insert from a furniture store. A medium-sized, half-empty laundry basket stands upstage left by an implied set of shelves and drawers. **Eunice** *sits in the stage left chair, leaning over with a Kevlar vest in both hands. She is dressed in muted active wear and a pair of slippers on her feet. A backpack and a single running shoe sit downstage right of her. Slight coughs and whimpers are heard from* **Eunice**; *these grow over the course of forty-five seconds, but never result in hysterical weeping.*

Eunice   Oh . . . oh . . . (*Draws breath audibly through a cry much like a donkey braying. Pauses. Clears throat. Shudders.*) Oooh . . .

Paballo *enters downstage left and pauses looking at* **Eunice** *for a few seconds and then proceeds into the kitchen. She is wearing a loose, floral button-up shirt and a chitenge wrapped around her waist. She carries a shopping bag with her that she places upon the table.*

Paballo   Somebody's being a selfish Susan, isn't she?

Eunice *does not respond. Pause.*

Paballo   I said, somebody's being . . .

Eunice   Perhaps I heard you and I was just trying to finish something.

Paballo   Started without me?

Eunice *pauses before they make eye contact.*

Eunice   I think between the two of us, there's only one of us whose waterworks need to be perfectly present.

Paballo   Ah, and that would be who exactly?

Eunice (*stresses*)   Whom.

Paballo (*laughs heartily*)   Gets you every time!

Eunice   It's only right that it *is* said right.

Paballo (*mockingly*)   Don't you sound like a mother.

Eunice   And a bloody good one at that. I'll be the first, second and even third to tell you.

Paballo   Now, now, Michelle Oh-*Baah*-ma. I was busy telling you that you started without me, let me have my moment.

Eunice   And I was telling you that I need to get my bits in before we get going.
I mean, you also left me here while you went off to do whatever it was you were doing. What were you doing?

Paballo   I had to pass by my nail girl before she closed for the evening and then helped old Mrs Molaledi into her bunker.

Eunice   Ah, Mama Mo, how is she doing?

Paballo   The best she can. Bones creak here, gas leaves there.

Eunice   Ha! Paballo!

Paballo   You asked how she was doing, I told you. Sue me. Anyway, how are the preparations?

Eunice   Emotionally, I think we're good. I should be able to give a nice convincing round or two. You? You're so dressed that no one would even imagine that you were going to take on the world.

Paballo   I couldn't exactly go out and about in battalion gear could I?

Starts to undress but realizes that she is missing undergarments. She digs in the laundry basket.

Eunice   Well, you know time is far from being on our side. Get to it.

Paballo   Yes, ma'am. (*She takes the laundry basket outside with her. Continues talking while offstage.*) And you're serious about me going after Lionel?

Eunice   Does my uterus still fight me on a regular basis?

Paballo   Yes, but . . .

Eunice   There are no buts in this. You take Lionel's no good ass out and I'll cover Nkamo.

Paballo   And the kids . . .

Eunice   Isn't that the very reason I have been doing this crying shit? Am I not readying myself for the kids? The kids who will, no doubt, be devastated by their father's death.

Paballo   Save the rage, madam, for the hunt. I was just confirming that you . . .

Eunice   What more do you need to confirm, Paballo? I said that this man deserves to go. I don't know why, when we've been given the complete authority to make that happen, you won't let me have my peace.

Paballo *enters with full basket and places it next to the upstage chair she sits in. She starts to undress and wear her muted active wear over her sports undergarments.*

Paballo   Hey. Hey. I'm the one who has to see the plan through, you can't bring him back to life once I've taken him out, so we have to be clear on these things.

Eunice   Take him all the way out. Him and that no good sedated eel he calls his pride and glory. (*She starts putting laces on her running shoes.*)

Paballo   Eel?!

Eunice   I guess it used to be, but now it's more of a salamander's tail or something. Now, that is one thing I wish I'd been taught as a young woman, 'Don't stay for the dick!'

Paballo   You thought you'd found love.

Eunice   What's that we used to call it?

Paballo   They still call it being *dickmatized*. (*They break out in laughter.*)

Eunice   It gave me two wonderful children that I love dearly and wouldn't replace for the world. But him and that thing, I need them to go. I need to start anew. And yes, I don't want him to be my ex-husband, I want to be widowed – you know how your people love a widow.

Paballo   Surely, as the elder, they're yours before they're mine.

Eunice   First, last, margarine or butter, the fact is they are yours and my statement remains the truth.

Paballo (*flips through the newspaper while putting on her shoes*)   Right, so this year's times have been set according to Jupiter's rising . . .

Eunice   You're starting . . .

Paballo (*laughs heartily*)   You are really so gullible it hurts. They're as basic as they were last year. (*Pause.*) Did you do anyone last year?

Eunice (*clears throat*)   Isn't that meant to remain a secret?

Paballo (*indignant*)   You're sending me out to go kill your husband. A father of three. Someone who regularly helps with emptying my skip when the council is slow to act. Someone who has submitted himself for candidacy for that very council.

Eunice   Opportunism becomes him, doesn't it?

Paballo   I'm just saying.

Eunice *walks over to* **Paballo**, *takes her by the shoulders first before begining to shake her. The shaking escalates as she speeds up. Her voice remains composed while sharp until erupting* . . .

Eunice   And what is Nkamo? Does your artistic language run pallid and dry when it comes to why she might need to stay around on this self-igniting planet? You simply see her in the office, she doesn't go home with you, sit there at birthday parties and drink with your family. Hell, she could forget your birthday year after year and you wouldn't care! God! I wish there were someone out there who was plotting my demise. Who knows, there might be. Someone hoping to quench their thirst for blood and peace by making me a figment of the past. Someone to relieve all the anxieties of tax and traffic and bills and betrayals and all this nonsense . . . NONSENSE!

She quivers, breathing shallow, and appears to break down into tears. **Paballo** *walks over to her and hugs her from behind. They hold the moment and then* **Eunice** *starts to shake more animatedly, eventually breaking out in laughter.*

Eunice   Yes! I've got it!

Paballo (*angrily slaps* **Eunice**'s *buttocks and returns to her shopping bag, from which she starts pulling out utensils and weapons*)   You FOOL. Or am I the fool? (*Laughs.*) No, you're right, you really do have it. Well done, my friend. *You* are eulogy ready!

Eunice   Thanks.

She walks over to the table to look through the weapons with which **Paballo** *has come back.*

Paballo   In addition to the batons and mini-Molotov cocktails . . .

Eunice   With the accompanying lighters, yes?

Paballo   Of course. But now shut up, it's my turn. We've got a pair of Swiss army knives, some cable ties, corkscrews in case the other ones don't come out properly, tranquilizing darts with straws, acid patches and spoons.

Eunice   Spoons?

Paballo   Yeah, how else do you expect to have your snacks? Bare handed? We're not barbarians.

Eunice   I just thought you were going all Matthew 5.29 on me . . . 'Weh, weh, weh, gouge out their eyes.'

They break out into hysterical laughter.

The End.

Interview with Sarah Dorgbadzi
by Ekua Ekumah
Legon Campus, University of Ghana,
5 February 2023

A conversation about the inaugural African Women Playwrights Network Festival, hosted by the School of Performing Arts, University of Ghana, in the Drama Studio, 1–4 September 2022.

Ekua   So, Dorgbadzi, I would like you to give a brief overview of how you came to be working on this African Women Playwrights Network Festival.

Sarah   Thank you very much. I first heard about the network at a School Management Committee meeting, where the Dean of the School of Performing Arts mentioned that the network was seeking to hold its maiden play reading festival and they were asking if the School of Performing Arts would be happy to host it, and I thought, 'Why not? This is a brilliant opportunity to see the world through windows opened by women, women talking about their world and their experiences; it's priceless. We are women, let us help our own.'

At the time, there were three women on the committee: the Head, Department of Music, Adwoa Arhine; the Artistic Director of Abibigromma, the Resident Theatre Company of the School of Performing Arts, Ekua Ekumah; and myself as the Head of the Department Theatre Arts, with me as the Chair of the Local Organizing Committee (LOC). We put our shoulders to the wheel, and then, *voilà*, we had a festival. So this is how I came to be in the picture.

Ekua   You were not only the Chair of the LOC for the festival, you were also at the first meeting with the rest of the steering committee members, who were 'Tosin Tume, Neo Kebiditswe, Philisiwe Twijnstra and Yvette Hutchison, who is the chair of the steering committee and the originator of this network. We put the task to direct the selected ten plays in your lap.

Sarah   Yes, I was determined to push all barriers and limitations to make this festival happen, if only to inspire another woman. I accepted the challenge to direct the ten selected plays.

One of the requests was to have a command performance as part of the programme for the festival, and we, as the host school, wanted to contribute something and showcase the work that is going on in the school, so as the directing lecturer I chose Efe Favour Uweribeno, one of my directing majors' one-act performance, which was about a woman talking about women's issues. I chose *Oro – The Reawakening* because of the story she told and because she was the only female directing major, and her play was questioning identity, and it was rooted in her culture, and it was also addressing taboo subjects, so her play fitted exactly the requirements for the plays that were going to be submitted.

Ekua   Before we move into your process, what was your initial response and conceptualization when you received the ten plays?

Sarah   I approached the plays with an open mind. I read all the ten plays just to hear the voices and what they were talking about, and to see what my instincts would tell me. I listen to my instincts a lot. As a director, I would be telling a story, and so I would like the plays to tell my story, and so that informed the choices and how I finally grouped the plays together, so that there's a clear pathway; there's a concept that is guiding the flow of the reading from one to the other. As I read the ten plays, I listened to my own responses, both as an individual and also an objective response. I don't know how to explain that, but I listened to myself and also read objectively removing self from the picture to see what the plays were communicating. For some of the plays, I felt a strong cultural, emotional, psychological connection. There were so many different levels of connection with the various plays. I must say that for some plays, I didn't have a personal response, but I had an intellectual response to them. I must say that once we brought the performers into the reading and their own interpretations came to the work, things began to shift, because it's a collaborative process, so the performers brought their input to the space, so some decisions had to be reconsidered and so I had to rearrange the jigsaw puzzle, and we arrived where we did.

Ekua   Can you tell me a little bit about the company that you set up. Where did they come from?

Sarah   I set up this company from a select group of students. Because we teach Directing and Acting, Ekumah and I drew on students; we also reached out to past students and National Service personnel. This is the company that we set up, and I must say that we all enjoyed working together beautifully; they all brought something to the bowl of salad.

Ekua   So now to talk about the plays proper. Can you talk us through the first three stories? In performance, our opening play was *Yanci*, and the second was *The Arrangement* and the third play is *A Woman Has Two Mouths*. Talk us through the journey or the subject matter of these plays and what made you decide to put them in this first segment.

Sarah   This segment actually is about marriage. Initially, the arrangement was different. It wasn't my personal decision; the company agreed to put *Yanci* first, which we saw as a good motivating message for young women who are facing opposition or are being ridiculed for one reason or the other in relation to their education. I felt that was a good strong message and a good note to start from; the whole thing about women emancipation, empowering a woman beyond religious and ethnic inhibitions and rules. We thought it was a moment of exhalation for today's young woman to be strong enough to stand up for their rights, and push the boundaries in society. These are initiators of change in our world today, so I found it a very strong piece, and so we made it the first one. Now, having said that, this woman is married and she's seeking to go against the odds in marriage, to step out there and be herself. We now went back to look into what goes into this marriage. What is this marriage that this woman is seeking to uphold, that her daughter must by all means live by the standards and the status quo? What is the marriage? So this brings us to the second play, *The Arrangement*. This marriage is an arrangement, where there is bargaining. The bargaining is being done by men over a woman, regardless of who or what she is, what her aspirations are, and in fact she was even rebuked, and her price reduced because of her education, and because she dared to say, 'No I'd like to have two children', but a woman must keep quiet.

Sarah   It's like an auction! She was being auctioned for cattle, and the cattle were being either increased for her positive things or decreased for what these men think were not of interest to them. The family of the man was deducting the cattle because she couldn't carry her pregnancies to term till finally they decided to nullify the marriage. And her husband . . .

Ekua   'Her partner in crime'. That's what she called him.

Sarah   Her partner in crime! Did he have any genuine affection for this woman or was she a piece of furniture he wanted to decorate his living room with, so that if the piece of furniture is no longer comfortable, then we can change it, or as the Americans would say, we chuck it out? Family had to come and do the chucking out, so that it will be public, and it will be super-embarrassing, and it would massage their egos, then they can feel like real men. Moving on from there, I imagine this woman having conversations with herself, and it was interesting and very emotional for me, because I know some young women who have been in that situation and some who still are in that situation. So I had emotional wells to draw from to fuel this woman's situation. Going on from here, we went on to *A Woman Has Two Mouths*, which is my way of imagining the details of the conversations she must have had with herself when she 'missed what she carried'. I have always been very particular about the philosophy of being, and the spirituality of life. This woman is talking about herself and her body, so that the self and the body in this context cease to be a unit; they're separate units, and so if they're separate units, then the self can be having conversations with the body and the body can be speaking from different parts and how they feel about what she's talking about, because at the end of the day, these body parts are directly responsible for holding, incubating and bringing out the baby she so much longs for, not just to please her man, but for self-fulfilment. She so much wanted to have this child, and that was another side of the conversation that I wanted to bring to the fore, that when women go through these things, there are various ways in which we should interrogate it, because I know personally, I've had conversations with parts of my body and encouraged my eyes, for example, to stay awake. I say, 'Eyes, I need you to stay open. I have to finish this work.' Forgive me if anyone finds this offensive: in the Bible, Paul says I have made a pact with my eyes that I may not sin by seeing. These are things I can directly relate to. I used to have painful ankles at a point and when I have to do certain tasks that I know are likely to bring up these pains, I would sit down and massage my legs and have this conversation with my legs, and say, 'Please see me through this thing.' It's just the way of life. Life has many layers and I particularly like the way that playwright spoke about it, and I liked the experience directing it. May I talk about that?

Ekua   Please, absolutely!

Sarah   The truth is I found it very interesting that, as women, we had inhibitions talking about our body parts. That was a very interesting, eye-opening experience for me. I had to tell stories upon stories, and sometimes when I'm telling these stories, the men in the company would leave the room because they find it embarrassing or uncomfortable, and sometimes the ladies playing the characters, for instance the main character, I told her to, 'Open your legs, and push that vagina forward and talk to her.' It took a while.

Ekua   What does that say about us as women?

Sarah   There are many dimensions to that. There's the cultural dimension where we have been socialized to stay compact. I remember being told that my vagina is where it is because it holds my future. If God in His own wisdom did not put it where it is, it would be easily accessible.

Ekua   It could be on your forehead.

Sarah   It could be on my forehead, but it is a sacred part of my body, because it is the part of my body that can bring another life into this world, and the fact that it can bring another life into this world requires that I take care of it, in terms of social life, cleanliness, and all the many things we can think of, so you don't make it public, don't expose your vagina. Cover your vagina, don't open it, and don't show it. It is not necessarily to demean it, but to hold it sacred, because it is a soil from which life will germinate, so it has to be kept well, well preserved and well protected. That is one side of the story. The other side of the story is our own inhibitions that we have come to build as a result of these cultural perceptions of the vagina. Yes, we should hold it sacred, but there's nothing wrong with me, as an individual, having conversations with my vagina. I know that women have a certain curiosity about what our bodies are. The feelings that come, the changes that come, menstrual cycles, the infections we get and how it feels, when you go to the hospital they want to test and all these things. How do we feel about it? These are some of the inhibitions that come up about this. The third thing yet is that, again, it's a growing up thing that when you talk about your vagina, you're labelled a bad girl.

Ekua   Yes that is it.

Sarah   And everybody has a special name for the vagina. We never get to say the actual name.

Ekua   It's down there; so many different names.

Sarah   So many different names. It all contributes to the constitution of how we relate to this sacred part of our body and the components that it entails.

Ekua   The playwright had two body parts: the vagina and the uterus. Can you comment a little about how the playwright represented those two body parts? The vagina was more comedic, and the uterus was melancholic, more emotional.

Sarah   I think for me, the way I understood that was most of the feelings that we get down there, we feel it in the vagina, if the feelings can be equated to emotions, all the emotions. And really, I don't know that we feel bad feelings there actually.

Ekua   Well, you can. As is stated in the play, they said in some parts of the world they clip you. Do you remember?

Sarah Yeah, but when they clip you, it's an infringement, but the natural feelings that come are pleasurable. It's a space for pleasure, and so I can clearly connect with the vagina being a bubbly, full of life, effervescent character. And you know, it has a very good memory. The vagina remembers the men that have made her feel good.

Ekua Yes, that was very interesting. And she was ambitious. I loved that.

Sarah She was. She could be a playwright or a poet or something interesting like that, a creative writer or something like that.

So at this point, the uterus is talking to the young woman, encouraging her to say, 'Do this and do that and let's get it right. You have been on too many birth control pills and this has an effect on me', so it was a way of drawing our attention to the choices that we make in our pre-productive years. We think of the moment. Again, I'm thinking for our young women and even for some older women too, we think of the moment, not realizing that the decisions we're making today have implications for what happens in the future. All these are details of the piece that I found very interesting and very inspiring. And so at the end of the play where the lady goes to sleep, I set the uterus's lines into a lullaby, because she's agitated emotionally, and she's directly in contact with the uterus, so if the uterus now can calm her down, then she finds peace. The lullaby can soothe her to sleep, because the woman must find life and continuity and energy in her own body.

Ekua That is profoundly beautiful. Thank you.

The second segment had three plays, *Who Is in My Garden*, *The Taste of Justice* and *Desperanza*. How did they follow on from segment one?

Sarah This segment, I put together to address abuse; abuse from another angle. In *Who Is in My Garden*, for instance, a woman leaves her house and her two grown-up daughters to her husband so she can go and find greener pastures, but what happens? The man gets busy raping her children. It is sexual abuse. I like the subject of the play. I dropped my son in school one day and I heard a group of class five girls talking, and one slapped the other's bum because she had passed a comment, and she quickly turned to rebuke her friend who slapped her bum, playfully, that, 'Hey, don't touch my bum oo, it belongs to my father.'

Ekua   Ei!

Sarah   Yes, she said that. And it caught my attention, so I followed up and went to speak to the school counsellor about this observation that I had made. The school counsellor said she will take it up and investigate the matter, but then she can only go as far as the girl would admit to her. That's it.

Ekua   'It belongs to my father.'

Sarah   'It belongs to my father.' So there are things going on. There are things happening. I just thought that was a very strong story to tell as well to warn unsuspecting young ladies. Growing up, I went to a girls' school and I have friends whose mothers' boyfriends were harassing them. I heard a lot of things like that. And so this is it with *Who Is in My Garden*. The next one, *The Taste of Justice*, is about an uncle who is abusing his orphaned nieces. And so the oldest of the three decides to free them from this bondage, and so she takes her revenge, using a kitchen knife and dismembered her abusive uncle and she enjoyed it, she says, and I would like to support her enjoyment. But now society turns around to call her names. Really?! Ibsen said, 'The strongest man is the one who stands alone.' I like the fact that she found strength to take this position, and didn't care a hoot what happened to her, but so long as her siblings were not going to be affected and the abuse had stopped, at least for the moment.

Moving on from there, we went to . . .

Ekua   *Desperanza*. The three sisters. The one I was in.

Sarah   Ah! So speak to it. How did you feel about it?

Ekua   Well I had an emotional connection to it because we're three sisters in my family, and at the time we even had some issues in the family so we were not as close as we had been. I was able to evoke the relationship that I have with my sisters and bring that to bear on this relationship. It was deeply felt for me. It was dealing with the issue of suicide. One of the sisters is on the verge of committing suicide and the older sister is calling, so there's this distance that exists between the two sisters who now have to deal with this issue right in front of each other; with just a door separating them. And then there's an older sister who is on the phone so I liked the idea of playing with distance in the piece and then having to deal with this heavy subject matter, but beautifully written in the way that it was. We moved from heavy, emotional matter to something really silly like beating someone in the shopping line with a 'gluten-free baguette'. It was a piece that I connected to immediately.

Sarah   So with this segment, clearly, you can see that it is something to do with siblings; family life, but from the perspective of siblings and sibling support and finding strength. I liked the idea of being so close and yet so far. It was a very sophisticated piece of material.

Ekua   I enjoyed that.

Sarah   And so that brought us to the end of day one.

Ekua   Six plays down.

Sarah   And so for day two, we had four longer plays and so they came in twos. So the first play for the morning session was *Oh!*

Ekua   *Oh!* was brilliant. And *In Her Silence*. Those were the two.

Sarah   You see, these two plays were talking about, again, sexuality in a way that is different from what has happened in the past. I put the two plays together so that we can look at them from two different perspectives: when the woman is able to talk about it and when the woman decides not to talk about it. In *Oh!* this woman goes to get for herself a sex toy, a vibrator. You know, she wants to have this relationship with her partner.

Ekua   It's interesting that she's not buying the sex toy to use personally; she wants her partner to use it on her, to pleasure her with the toy, which is quite a bold move!

Sarah   Exactly!

Ekua   Very bold.

Sarah   And only to find out that man felt belittled that his wife would bring him a toy, because he has his weapons in the proper places and in the optimum condition, and so he doesn't see why. But really, is it just about him?

Ekua   That is it.

Sarah   That is it. Is it just about what he's giving? And what if what he is giving is

Both   Not enough!

Sarah   And so is it wrong? So he decides not to give and not to use what has been provided and goes off to sleep. I felt like changing the end of the play, so that she can turn around and use it on herself to his hearing, but then I didn't have the liberty to do that.

Ekua   It was interesting after the play reading, the discussions that came up; I found that very revealing on the audience who were listening. I think we had a split. There were those who said, 'Oh, she should just put that thing away', and there were those who said, 'You're not listening to what the woman is saying.' It was interesting that some of our young men were the ones who were advocating that the woman should have used it. Damn him, you know, and she should pleasure herself. If you're not going to, I have the tool, I've paid for it. It's mine so let me use it. I found that very refreshing that it was a discovery for young men.

Sarah   You know the interesting thing, the relationship I had with this play, which is that I have a friend whose husband travels around a lot. It is her husband who bought the vibrator for his wife.

Ekua   Wow.

Sarah   And he bought the vibrator to match his size.

Ekua   Ei! Wow. So when he's away . . .

Sarah   She can pleasure herself.

Ekua   That is very forward thinking. Wow.

Sarah   And then in our conversations when one of our friends was saying that her husband is being very mean and all that, she said, 'Charley, then you can pleasure yourself.' And that is how I got to know. And she brought it.

Ekua   Oh wow.

Ekua   Mhmm. Then we move on to *In Her Silence*. This is our only Ghanaian representation in the festival.

Sarah   Yes. *In Her Silence* is the side of the story where this woman has decided, that unlike the first one who openly talks to her husband and prepares a presentation to entice him, she has decided that she's going to be silent. Her weapon was her silence. The man does everything and she is just silent, and the frustration was admirable. I just loved it. In my perception of things, the whole play was controlled by the woman's silence, and her silence is being spoken. According to the text, the silence is a representation of her thoughts, her responses to the man's pronouncement were subtitled and projected on a screen. but then technically we weren't going to be able to do it, because these plays were being done during the day in an open-air space so we were not going to be able to have an effective use of a projector. And so I decided to get the words spoken. And so I chose a voice that had so much presence within the company. A voice that can override the voice of the husband, so that that voice, which is her silence, is so loud that it manipulates the man's everything and frustrates him so much to show how much power there is in silence, and again the contradiction is that this silence is voiced in silence. Now, there was the issue about a man's voice; that the voice that was sounding was a man's voice, but then in today's world, the issue of man's voice, woman's voice is really very complex, especially since we have other persons in this team of women. So what is a man's voice? Voice is sound, and I didn't think that sound was gendered. If I had brought a presence into the space, you'll see what looks to you as a man but they could pronounce themselves woman. All these dynamics are at play. So this one, I didn't think much of it. I didn't think that voice which is sound was gendered, so I chose a voice that would play what the concept was, but it came across to people as a man's voice and they wanted a woman's voice and all this conversation but this is it.

Ekua   Then that ends the morning session. We're now into the evening session of the last day of reading. *Horny & . . .*, our South African contribution, and then *Gnash* from Botswana. Southern Africa took up the tail end of our play reading. Talk us through *Horny & . . . .*

Sarah   You played in *Horny & . . .* How did you feel?

Ekua   Hmmm, *Horny & . . .* I remember . . .

Sarah   Let me just say this before I forget. My thing about *Horny & . . .* was how very well it represented the way I speak.

Ekua   Oh really? Interesting.

Sarah   Yes. My husband always says, 'Why don't you ever say something straight and finish it?' Because I start one thing and then I remember something else to elaborate this story and in the elaboration I bring something else to elaborate that story that must elaborate this one, and then I go and then I come back to it. I keep going in and out. All that, in my mind, is to make the story more explicit. So I found *Horny & . . .* amazing. It lent itself to theatre of the postmodern.

Ekua   Yes, absolutely. I remember when we first read it in your office, we said, we'll not do this. Remember?

Sarah   Yes.

Ekua   Because she was also graphic. She was unapologetically graphic. Or maybe graphic is not the word, but honest about her sexuality, how she engages with her body, how she talks about her vagina and her breasts in a way that other plays hadn't. So it was a bit of a 'Whoo, this is where we are' and we needed some time to hear it for it to become normal, Yes, I felt that, but upon reading it, it was heavy as well. It was a heavy subject matter.

Sarah   Yes, so the thing about my initial reaction was that it was written for a lone voice.

It was almost thirty minutes. We needed to do some cuts and turn things around to make it work. And so directorially, to make it less heavy, I gave it to two voices, so I put two women in the space to interact. So the whole thing is about the dialogue of the splitting of the same mind. So that it became more accommodating in that sense. Otherwise, I think it was a brilliant piece. I loved it.

Ekua Yes. It was very strong, very honest, graphic and challenging.

Sarah Yes, allows you room to do a lot.

Ekua Yes, yes, yes. So from a performer's point of view, I felt challenged at some points. I felt a little inhibited at some points, and some moments, I just felt like an advocate. I needed to speak these words so that these stories are shared, so that whoever might be going through this 'know you're not alone'. All these feelings were going on for me. Very strong.

Sarah Very, very, very strong.

Ekua Then we ended with *Gnash*.

Sarah Two friends, planning to murder each other's husbands.

Ekua Actually, the interesting thing about this is they were supposed to be fifty-plus-year-old women, so actually it should have been us, but it was just too much going on. But I think we would have given it a different interpretation if we had read it. But speak to this play.

Sarah This play is about two women who have come to the point where they say, 'Enough is enough.' And I know I have read about a certain group of people who took pride in being a widow instead of a divorcee.

Ekua Yes, that is it.

Sarah And so that is the connection I had with this story. I didn't have any particular emotional or cultural connection to this story's experience. It was on an intellectual level. They're deciding that they'll take them out, and they're doing it unapologetically, and they're even rehearsing how they're going to play out the mourning so that they can cover up so people will not know that they did it deliberately.

Ekua   Yes, there's something I found interesting about this that even having women of that age, you often don't find plays about women of that age group, so I found that refreshing that this generation who have lived, they're probably grandmothers and things, but they've reached a stage where they think like actually, 'This is the time I should be enjoying myself but I've still got "baggage" that I'm pulling around, baggage that doesn't realize what I'm doing. Let me cut it loose.' So there was something liberating about these women of a certain generation who have come to a realization about their own value and are not waiting for anybody to give them permission to come into their own, so there was something revolutionary about it.

Sarah   Very revolutionary. Actually, come to think of it, it's interesting that we're having this conversation now. Only yesterday, last night, a friend of mine whose husband has had a stroke and is recovering, has taken a certain turn. You know when people have a stroke there's a turn where they call it the confusion state, and things like that. This man has been a verbally abusive husband since Adam was a toddler, and now he's getting to a point where he's punching my friend, he's hitting her, calling her names, she's a witch.

Ekua   Even in his condition?

Sarah   Even in his condition now. And her children are up in arms and saying, 'Ma, this is not illness, this is his behaviour. This is his character.' And my friend is saying, 'Enough is enough. I am not going to do anything about it. He can do whatever he likes. When he dies, we will bury him.' When we had this conversation, this is the play I remembered. Only she's not initiating the death, but she's not going to be looking anymore for healing, because it's not bringing any satisfaction, she might as well enjoy her life and leave him to be. Wow.

Ekua   Wow, indeed.

Sarah   Women's issues.

Ekua   Yes. So that brings us to the end of *Gnash*.

Sarah   Yeah. And I wanted to say that in dealing with these plays, I wasn't quite sure as a director whether I was supposed to be doing it as a command performance or I should stay true to the text. I didn't know how much liberty the director was supposed to have in this, but I kept telling myself, if it's a play reading, then let's stay as true to the text as possible so that we can see what needs to be reworked, what the strengths and weaknesses are, but then again, at the same time, there were points where I couldn't help straying a bit.

Ekua   You're working with a concept.

Sarah   Yes, just to make the process enjoyable. So apologies to all those who felt I have not been truthful to their plays, but actually, on the whole, it was a great experience. Thank you for bringing it. We did enjoy working on that.

Ekua   We did indeed. Thank you very much.

Further reading

Other ten-minute plays

It is interesting that a lot of these short plays have been aimed at children, fewer at older persons and Black women. The majority of students doing drama degrees are female, so we hope this collection speaks to a gap regarding the African perspective, including diasporas.

Daley-Sharif, Sandra A. 2018. *10-Minute Plays Anthology Presented by Harlem9, Inc.: 48Hours in . . .* ™ *Harlem Volume 2*. (Aimed at 14–18-year-olds, this is an anthology of plays by twelve new and emerging Black playwrights, presented by the OBIE Award-winning Harlem9, Inc., presenters of the annual 48Hours in. . .™ Harlem Festival.)

Griffith, Carlene M. 2016. *10 Minute Plays for Kids of All Ages*: Volumes 1 & 2. (For 6–20 characters.)

Harbison, Lawrence (ed.) 2018. *The Best Ten-Minute Plays 2017*. Hanover, NH: Smith & Kraus.

Collections of plays by African women

Perkins, Kathy (ed.) 2009. *African Women Playwrights*. Urbana, IL: University of Illinois Press.

Hutchison, Yvette and Amy Jephta. 2019. *Contemporary Plays by African Women*. London: Bloomsbury Methuen Drama.

African play collections

Banham, Martin and Jane Plastow (eds) 1999. *Contemporary African Plays*. London: Methuen.

Hutchison, Yvette and Kole Omotoso. 1995. *Open Space: An Introduction to African Drama*. Cape Town: Kagiso.

Jeyifo, Biodun (ed.) 2002. *Modern African Drama*. New York: Norton & Co.

Secondary reading on women and gender in Africa

Bennett, Jane and Charmaine Pereira (eds) 2013. *Jacketed Women –
    Qualitative Research Methodologies on Sexualities and Gender in
    Africa.* Claremont: University of Cape Town Press.

Cole, Catherine, Takyiwaa Manuh and Stephan F. Miescher (eds) 2007.
    Africa after Gender? Bloomington, IN: Indiana University Press.

Connell, R. W. '2005. Hegemonic Masculinity – Rethinking the Concept'.
    Gender & Society, 19:6, 829–59.

Connell, R. W. 1995. *Masculinities*. Cambridge: Polity Press.

Farfan, Penny and Lesley Ferris. 2013. *Contemporary Women
    Playwrights: Into the Twenty-first Century*. Basingstoke: Palgrave
    Macmillan.

Flockemann, Mikki. 1998. 'Women, Feminism and South African
    Theatre'. In L. Goodman and J. De Gay (eds), *The Routledge Reader in
    Gender and Performance*. London: Routledge, 218–22.

Gouws, Amanda (ed.) 2005. *(Un)thinking Citizenship: Feminist Debates
    in Contemporary South Africa*. Aldershot: Ashgate Publishers.

Hutchison, Yvette. 2013. *South African Performance and the Archives of
    Memory*. Manchester: Manchester University Press.

Hutchison, Yvette. 2019. *Woza Africa! An Educational Toolkit on Theatre
    in the African Context*, register to download at Woza Africa! (warwick.
    ac.uk).

James, Adeola. 1990. *In Their Own Voices: African Women Writers Talk*.
    Oxford: James Currey.

Marzette, DeLinda. 2013. *Africana Women Writers: Performing Diaspora,
    Staging Healing*. New York: Peter Lang.

Mekgwe, Pinkie. 2007. 'Theorizing African Feminism(s) – the Colonial
    Question', in Tobias Robert Klein, Ulrike Auga and Viola Prüschenk
    (eds), *Texts, Tasks, and Theories: Versions and Subversions in African
    Literatures*, Vol. 3. Amsterdam: Rodopi, 165–214.

Mikell, Gwendolyn. 1997. *African Feminism*. Philadelphia: University of
    Pennsylvania Press.

Morell, Robert (ed.) 2001. *Changing Men in Southern Africa (Global
    Masculinities)*. London: Zed Books

Nnaemeka, Obioma (ed.) 1988. *Sisterhood – Feminisms and Power from
    Africa to the Diaspora.* Trenton, NJ: Africa World Press.

Plastow, Jane (ed.) 2002. *African Theatre: Women*. Oxford: James Currey.

Plastow, Jane, Yvette Hutchison and Christine Matzke (eds) 2015. *African
    Theatre 14: Contemporary Women*. Woodbridge: James Currey.

Tamale, Sylvia (ed.) 2011. *African Sexualities – A Reader*. Oxford: Pambazuka Press.

Useful readings on African Theatre

Banham, Martin (ed.) 2004. *A History of Theatre in Africa*. Cambridge: Cambridge University Press.

Banham, Martin, James Gibbs and Femi Osofisan. *African Theatre: Playwrights & Politics*. Oxford: James Currey, 1999.

Barber, K, J. Collins and A. Ricard. 1997. *West African Popular Theatre*. Oxford: James Currey.

Boon, R. and J. Plastow. 1998. *Theatre Matters*. Cambridge: Cambridge University Press.

Breitinger, E. (ed.) 1998. *Theatre and Performance in Africa*. Bayreuth African Studies 31.

Conteh-Morgan, John and Tejumola Olaniyan. 2004. *African Drama and Performance*. Bloomington, IN: Indiana University Press.

Dunton, C. 1992. *Make Man Talk True: Nigerian Drama in English Since 1970*. London: Hans Zell Publishers.

Etherton, M. 1982. *The Development of African Drama*. New York: Africana.

Fanon, F. 1986. *Black Skin, White Masks*. C. L. Markmann, trans. London: Pluto Press.

Fanon, F. 1963. *The Wretched of the Earth*. Preface by J.-P. Sartre. New York: Grove Press.

Gibbs, J. 1986. *Wole Soyinka*. Basingstoke: Macmillan.

Gunner, L. (ed.) 1994. *Politics and Performance: Theatre, Poetry and Song*. Johannesburg: Witwatersrand University Press.

Igweonu, Kene and Osita Okagbue (eds) 2013. *Performative Inter-Actions in African Theatre 3: Making*. Newcastle-upon-Tyne: Cambridge Scholars Publishing.

Igweonu, Kene (ed.) 2011. *Trends in Twenty-First Century African Theatre and Performance*. Amsterdam: Rodopi.

Kerr, D. 1995. *African Popular Theatre*. Cape Town: David Phillip.

Kerr, David. 1998. *Dance, Media-Entertainment, and Popular Performance in South East Africa*. Bayreuth: Eckhard Breitinge.

Kruger, Loren. 1999. *The Drama of South Africa*. London: Routledge.

Lindfors, B. (ed.) 1980. *Critical Perspectives on Nigerian Literatures*. Washington, DC: Three Continents Press.

Losambe, Lokangaka and Devi Sarinjeive (eds) 2001. *Pre-Colonial and Post-Colonial Drama and Theatre in Africa*. Claremont: New Africa Books.

Mda, Zakes. 1993. *When People Play People: Development Communication Through Theatre*. London: Zed Books.

Mudimbe, V. Y. 1988. *The Invention of Africa: Gnosis, Philosophy and the Order of Knowledge*. London: James Currey.

Ogunbiyi, Y. 1981. *Drama and Theatre in Nigeria: A Critical Source Book*. Lagos: Nigeria Magazine.

Olaniyan, T. 1995. *Scars of Conquest/Masks of Resistance – the Invention of Cultural Identities in African, African-American, and Caribbean Drama*. New York: Oxford University Press.

Plastow, Jane. 1996. *African Theatre and Politics: the Evolution of Theatre in Ethiopia, Tanzania and Zimbabwe*. Amsterdam: Rodopi.

Richards, S. L. 1996. *Ancient Songs Set Ablaze: The Theatre of Femi Osofisan*. Washington, DC: Howard University Press.

Schipper, Mineke. 1982. *Theatre and Society in Africa*. Johannesburg: Ravan.

Soyinka, W. 1976. *Myth, Literature and the African World*. London: Cambridge University Press.

wa Thiong'o, Ngugi. 1993. *Moving the Centre*. London: James Currey.

wa Thiong'o, Ngugi. 1986. *Decolonising the Mind*. London: James Currey.

Useful journals

Agenda
Research in African Literatures
South African Theatre Journal